C000060313

Kid on a Red C
A ride through the 1970's

By Tony Beesley

Best wishes

Tony Beesley

Printed on FSC approved paper by

FASTPRINT GOLD PUBLISHING

PETERBOROUGH, ENGLAND

In memory of Mum and Dad

Kid on a Red Chopper Bike
Copyright © Tony Beesley 2011

All publishing rights and copyright owned by the author Tony Beesley
'Days like Tomorrow Books'

All rights reserved.

No part of this book may be reproduced in any form by
photocopying or any electronic or mechanical means,
including information storage or retrieval systems,
without permission in writing from both the copyright
owner and the publisher of the book.

ISBN 978-0-9565727-2-1

First Published 2011 by 'Days like Tomorrow books'

Printed by
FASTPRINT GOLD PUBLISHING
Peterborough, England.

Cover designed by Dave Spencer

www.printondemand-worldwide.com

Contents

Press quotes

"It's a real love letter to Tony's childhood and roots, and even though I'm ten years older than him it triggered many memories. I really enjoyed it."... Garry Bushell - Daily Star

"Kid on a Red Chopper Bike is a great romp through the decade. You'll relive the 70's but will also relive your childhood – I would challenge you not to..." ... Sally Burton - South Yorkshire Times

"It's a mix of the mundane and madness, triumph and tragedy, fun and nostalgia. If you are too young to have lived through the 70's, you will wish you had been there."... John Quinn - Sheffield Star

Introduction

"I just had to have a Red Chopper bike; it was the coolest thing ever for a ten year old and was the most wanted thing in my life so far... I really could not imagine not being able to ride one of my own."

The 1970's ('Confessions' and saucy 'Carry On' films, a big fat Greek singer in a dress and the Grumbleweeds); supposedly the decade when all sense of cool fashion and good taste got thrown out of the window! Well, that's easy to proclaim in hindsight. For me, it was a time of fun, colour, excitement, learning and the freedom of being a kid growing up without the restrictions of previous times or the suffocation of modern day PC-rules and fearful thinking. It was a time of discovery, innocence, making mistakes and obsession: of experiencing a decade that could never be relived again. A time when kids were allowed to be kids and given the space to be so; we had little money, gadgets or trendy gear... but we had our imaginations. I grew up during those days: let me tell you something about it all!

Please let me introduce myself! I am that young Punk kid in the 'Our Generation' trilogy of books: the one who was crazy about The Jam and The Clash and revelled in sticking two fingers up at the system and my peers. Those years were a time of unsurpassable energy and excitement at a pivotal time of my growing up. The attitude I carried around fit the Punk ideal like a glove and helped shape me into the person I am today. Before those years of rebellion and the consequent years of Post-Punk frustration, my story was one of a quieter rebellion, but one still directed at a choice selection of adults... and yes teachers!

This story (a sort of prequel to my story in 'Our Generation') goes back to the end of the swinging sixties and my unwanted introduction to school life and follows my begrudged school years journey through the groovy, long-haired seventies, with a dip into the culture, history and the in things and must haves of the day along the way! It's a story of a kid, like many others, not knowing what was gonna happen next... it's a funny little story with some funny people in it and hardly ever takes itself too seriously. It's most likely to be not that much different to a whole generation of kids stories of the time, but the difference is that I have bothered to write about it all: its special to me, though, and I think it's worth re-visiting and worth a chuckle and memory jog to you too!

The generation of kids I knew, and often hung around with, offered a whole chocolate box of character flavours.... Or more like a lucky bag of bitter-sweet sherbet-sucking swine's. I grew up alongside kids at school who turned out to be musicians, Head teachers, firemen, taxi drivers, armed robbers, drug addicts and kids who sadly took their own lives or who died tragically young. There were good and bad kids, honest and dishonest... funny and serious ones, troubled kids, happy go lucky kids... we all turned out different to each other and to what each of us expected of the other... but back then we all had one thing in common... we had a childhood to experience!

Before I reached my teenage Punk Rock destination almost at the end of the decade, I was living the part of a young and incredibly innocent, yet compulsively mischievous youngster. I was a WW2-obsessed, Airfix Model-making, school-dodging, comic-buying, and hide and seek-loving kid on a red Chopper bike! Yet, I was not alone within this magical 'six weeks school holiday worshipping' world where summer seemed to always be red hot and bright whilst winters meant real proper snow. Days when if you lipped a copper you had to make sure you were a bloody good runner and teachers could still give you a damned good hiding without serving time at Her Majesty's pleasure. An era now seeming almost to have never even existed times have changed so much. But those days did happen and if you can catch me on my red chopper bike... I'll tell you the tale of those days of fun, daftness, lad's comics and toys, Spangle sweets and school kid mischievousness. It's not all bright and breezy... but it's a story worth telling. So all you big over-grown kids - lads and lasses, swots, toughs, classroom clowns and teachers pets too, let's get in our Tardis and go back and re-live our childhood dreams and past. Let's have a ride on that Chopper Bike once more... You know you want to be there!

Chapter One

Early Days

I was born at Rotherham Moorgate hospital on June 12th 1965 to parents George Kenneth Beesley – known as Ken (a miner at Kilnhurst colliery from the age of 14 who had been brought up at Claypit Lane, Rawmarsh) and Eileen Shaw (who had resided with her six brothers and one sister on Goosebutt Street, Parkgate). My parents had met towards the end of the Second World War; My Dad (who had a brother and one sister) followed in the footsteps of a list of male admirers, including a fella in the Irish guards and at one point an American GI who pleaded for my Mother's hand only to be turned down to make way for my dad.

Watching the box! Our Paul, Mother and (at the rear) my Grandma (Mother's side) and Aunty Irene at Goosebutt Street early 1950's. A typical Post-War scene captured on photo

These innocent war time romances would soon make way for a more serious *you made your bed now lie in it* young marriage that would finally bring about a family life in a semi-detached house on Warren Avenue in the newly built area of Monkwood, Rawmarsh with my two elder brothers Paul (born 1947) and Glen (born 1954). Stories of those early days on Warren Avenue would pass into our family folklore.

Above –Uncle Jack (one of Mum's brothers) serving in India in WW2... one of my other Uncles (Bill) served in North Africa and Italy where he was wounded in action and left for dead

Above right - My Bingo-loving Mother with our Paul (1947)

Tales of my Mum having to force our Paul to go to school (one successful attempt saw him return trooping up the street looking all smart, uncharacteristically clean and proper – and turning around with no back in his brand new school blazer), of scarf-wearing Mothers battling over the warring kids and my pissed up Dad trying to climb the door to get upstairs to bed. Join these with mesmerising and ear-catching stories of the war years (my Mum worked in a munitions factory in Tinsley and was there when the Jerries blitzed Sheffield in 1940 and had two brothers, Jack and Bob serving overseas), and there were plenty of tales to tell.

Many of those wartime tales are, sadly, now long-forgotten; since almost all of the people in them are no longer with us. My passed-down memories of those stories are quite hazy now. I recall stories told of the German and Italian prisoners of war building the Rawmarsh cemetery wall and as my Mum and friends passed them by, those young fellas whistling and blowing kisses at them. On my enquiring of "What did they look like Mum?"... my war-obsessed little mind hoping for a reply of something like "They were Nazi monsters and deserved shooting" or that they actually did get mowed down by a well-aimed Bren gun post, I was quite surprised to hear Mum say "They were just like any of our young lads, no different, just different uniforms and thinner and sadder faces." Apparently, still to this day, there are some messages/signatures from the prisoners hidden away on the bottom wall of that cemetery, though I have never been able to find them. My Mum could tell a really good story and listening to these wartime ones really brought to life those days gone by, forever implanting in my mind a vision of how it must have been during those years of rationing, air raids and war.

Mum was in Morecambe, working as a young house-helper/cleaner doing her service days in a hotel when war broke out. She and her sister, my Auntie Amy, were summoned straight home, almost. Her experience of hearing the famous Chamberlain speech of the declaration of war between us and Germany was in that hotel in Morecambe and within the last few days she spent there, the town was turned into a prospective defence line of barbed wired-beaches, forbidden zones and countless amounts of soldiers passing through.

Following a family argument, as a matter of rebellion against his parents, my Mum's brother, my Uncle Bill, signed up in the forces. His wartime journey sent him over to North Africa with Monty's Desert Rats and onto Italy. Whilst on campaign in Italy, Bill's company drank from a town's well for over a day or so, only to find a dead German float to the top afterwards. According to Bill's relaying of information to my Mum, it hardly ever stopped raining for most of the time he served over in so-called sunny Italy.

In 1944, following hard campaigning and fierce battles, Bill's company were ambushed and wiped out to the man. Severely wounded, Bill waved in and out of consciousness and through a haze of pain; shock and blurred vision saw the Germans arrive to a scene of the slaughtered remains of the British soldiers and their vehicles. The enemy then proceeded to bayonet all of the dead and wounded to make sure there were no survivors. Bill received a bayonet in the neck to add to his chest wound and, along with the rest of the soldiers, was left for dead. He survived to tell the tale. No-one else did. Most people in Mum's family agree that Bill was a much more reserved and quieter person on his return from the war. My other Uncle, Jack, served in India. Bringing home exotic Indian silk garments and scarves for his sisters on a first aid boat after a wound fighting the Japanese, they were stopped by a German U-Boat who boarded the ship to inspect it. No-one was harmed, but everything that they had with them was taken away from them and thrown into the sea.

Mum served at Tinsley Wire which doubled as a munitions factory and also produced dummy tanks for use to fool the Germans prior to D-Day. She had been working there a year or so when the Germans decided to bomb Sheffield. She told me of that night. She was working as the sirens began. After hours of bombing over in the city, they were all sent home. It was pitch-black, except for the glare of fires burning in Sheffield and Mum and her friends struggled to make their way home as the bombing intensified. Luckily she was picked up by an army truck making its way into Rotherham and managed to arrive home safely.

My Dad wasn't allowed to serve in the forces as he worked down the pit in a reserved occupation. Whether he attempted to sign up and was refused or not, I don't know. My Dad never let on much of his younger days, but I wouldn't be surprised if he did try. His contribution, however, to the war effort was travelling miles underground into red hot claustrophobic tunnels containing minimal oxygen and little light and shovelling black coal for war fuel. Towards the end of the war, most likely just prior to D-Day, Dad met my Mum and managed to persuade her to pack in the American GI she was seeing and take him on instead. The rest is history, so the saying goes!

Those black and white days of 1940's wartime hardship and 1950's working class kinship and trouble and strife kept me interested during many a power cut blackout in the 1973 strikes or belting thunder storms when every item of electricity would be switched off in case of lightning infiltration. But, those days had passed when this mistake of a kid arrived on the scene during the so called swinging sixties, an era I was born right in the middle of, but grew up blissfully unaware of its significance!

A right gang of 1960's seaside dwellers in 1965... our Glen, Dad, Mum, Aunty Amy and kids and friends and Uncle Eric at the back...I am in my Mum's belly

The youngest of three sons (my elder sister to be- Dawn sadly died at birth some years previously), apparently I entered this upside down world - well upside down and choking on the umbilical cord; a shade of ghastly purple from the lack of oxygen. My later years of restlessness, irrationality and general unexplainable stupidness and unpredictability may well have been rooted in that very day's birthing calamity - who knows?

Copyright the Francis Frith Collection

A view of part of the Rawmarsh shopping centre in 1965 looking towards
the top of Rawmarsh Hill and the Church. The market stalls shown later
moved further up, where a small amount still remain, whilst the area
shown here is now parking space.

The village of Rawmarsh – in itself a suburb of Rotherham – was first mentioned as Rodemesc in the Doomsday book. Also referred to as Rubeo Marisco, Routhemersk and Romerssh throughout the years, finally ending up as Rawmarsh as its official title in tribute to its local's past pronunciation of Romush or Romish. Other histories state that the name is in homage to its Red soil (Redmarsh is the name of one avenue in the village).

Originally a scattering of dwellings based around the High Street, Dale Road and Stocks Lane area, the 1900's saw the introduction of mining and the village increasing vastly in size and population. Prior to Rawmarsh being integrated into the Rotherham Borough Council, the village did have its very own separate council. The Monkwood area of Rawmarsh (so named after the Monk's Monastery that was situated in the woods in the vicinity of where the Monkwood Junior school is now), where I was brought up was built in the early 1950's and, along with the rest of the village continued its growth right throughout that decade and beyond.

In the middle of the sixties a shopping centre was built in the village, off Stocks Lane and parallel to Dale Road, complete with a bingo (my Mother's dream come true) which took over the old cinema building (the other cinema just over the road had been called Robby's and stories of Kid's matinees there would be recited by family and friends over the years). Some other shops were joined by a small toy shop called Schofield's right in the bottom corner, which later turned to selling wool instead of Airfix kits and the like, but not before I had raided it for some Union infantry.

The shopping centre was only about half a mile from where we lived, but visits there on a Friday morning were classed as a mini day out. It had an outdoor market on a Friday too, so was worth the trawl. I have some very early memories of going to the shopping centre, many of them involving being dragged into the bingo by my Mother and her bribing me with a cheap plastic racing car or the Eagle 1968 annual to stay quiet while she lit a fag and took her game seriously- glaring daggers at the other hardcore bingo gang when they said the words "Pull!" "Don't tell yer Dad when he comes in from work Tony" she would say. For some unknown reason, at the time, my Mother hardly told my Dad if she was going to the bingo (but then again he didn't tell her where he had been on the piss half the time either):

it was all hush hush as I later discovered he would cut her house-keeping money down if he thought she was wasting it in the bingo. Plus, when she had a good win, the dividends would be a greater profit margin for her. Occasionally he would ask her if she had been to the bingo (or Bongo as she called it!), to her negative reply. He would say "Oh that's funny as Bill's wife has told him (and the entire pit) that you had a good win yesterday?" A firm denial would ensue followed by a damn good row.

My Dad was a complete torment. Each Saturday he would be met with pleas from my Mum to not take the mickey out of our Glen on his return from the Rotherham Utd match (usually a lost game). She knew he couldn't help himself and our Glen took his team and football very seriously. Understandably he would take it to heart when the team failed to meet expectations. Predictably my Dad would wait intently for the results and his face would light up when he knew he had something to gloat over. Each week he would promise my Mum that he wasn't going to say a word.

It became a weekly ritual. As soon as Glen came through the door, before he could even take his shoes off, my Dad's face would light up, the grin clearly betraying his intent. I would wait and count the seconds down. I loved the taste of the torment too: I had received high quality training from my family members. "What have them clowns been up to today then, Glen?" would open up the attack. "I'd ask how you had gone on at the football, but seeing as Rotherham don't play football I won't ask." These would continue: My mum cursing him, our Glen furious and banging away at cupboards, me chuckling like Mutley on the settee. One of the gifts Dad handed me down, was an ability to torment and take the mickey – out of myself if need be too, though that particular twist to the art of the torment didn't stretch to my Dad's sense of humour. In short he could give it, but it wasn't hard to wind him up either... an inroad that our Paul swiftly recognised. Much of the percentage of our family's past is taken up with taking the piss and/or subsequent sessions of rowing and falling out. It's a family gift you see!

In later years, when my Dad was ill, he would torment my Mother by letting her think she had to stop in and at the very last minute throw some money at her and say "here Eileen, get yourself to the bingo." Her face would light up, brush and rouge out and ready in five minutes flat she would be off. I would be getting the soldiers out and saying "Right Dad, seeing as its me and you, which side of soldiers do you think is going to win the battle" as the toy box was emptied on the floor. Dad would sit and watch as I re-enacted battle after battle and when I passed some Timpo bits and pieces he would piece them together for me: those memories are happy ones for me. It took my Dad to start to take ill for me to get some much-yearned proper time with him, but it was great!

Me, the Monkey and my Dad sometime in the swinging sixties in Scarborough

My year of birth, 1965, was a fairly eventful year, so I am told and have since discovered. The decade was well on its path to being a swinging one as the beat boom exploded further, the Beatles went serious, the Rolling Stones yearned some Satisfaction, Folk/Rock was born with Dylan going electric releasing his influential 'Bringing it all back Home' album. and the Byrds found his 'Mr Tambourine Man.' Mod went further public: protests were on the agenda against Vietnam and the whole climate of the world was changing. Sir Winston Churchill and Stan Laurel both passed away in a year that saw The Who unleash their 'My Generation' anthem and long player, along with the assassination of Malcolm X, the first walk in space (Russian Cosmonaut Aleksei Leonov left his spacecraft for a whole twelve minutes) and the banning from British TV of cigarette advertising.

My earliest memories are a little mixed up, as can be expected: As that lovable thin fella Stan Laurel once answered when asked "Can you remember when you were born?" - "I'm not sure; I can't quite remember, I was too young!" So as is usually the case, mine - like most other people's earliest memories are hazy, vague and most likely not all in perfect and exact order.

My Dad was a pit man through and through. He worked hard with a set of 'loyal to the death' mates miles under the ground and while up back on earth he loved to be with those very mates in a good boozer. He was smart, proud and hard (Try surviving a pit accident all those miles down when the lot caved in on him and if not for his damn good mates digging and pulling him out, he would have been a goner... his injuries included no flesh left on his back and two front teeth knocked straight up his nose... try surviving that and then go back down there again).

Below: Dad and right: Mum playing up for the camera

Dad had only one brother, my Uncle Dennis, who we all know more commonly as Uncle Nip. Nip had a bit of a dodgy leg and had to wear callipers when he was a kid. Of course, he got picked on cos of that and my Dad used to look after him and belt any kids that picked on him. That was his nature, my Dad: he hated anyone being the underdog. He lived a life of mates and the pit and the boozer, though never touched a drop at home, and firmly believed in morals and codes of conduct, or something like that.

I think he was also a classic product of the golden age of 1930's film matinees. As kids he and his mates would go and watch the Hopalong Cassidy films, Flash Gordon, gangster films starring his favourite actor and gangster James Cagney who my dad truly believed was a real person in his film roles. In Dad's eyes, no-one was tougher than James Cagney and would often quote him from his films "You dirteee rat." He also loved John Wayne, Ward Bond (these were real men) and the Welsh mining village-set John Ford film 'How Green was my Valley' held legendary status to him. So did 'Gone with the Wind' ('They can't make films like that any more' he would argue) and 'Angels with Dirty Faces.' All the things that his film heroes believed in, being tough, right, strong, defending the under-dog and not least, being clean and smart in appearance... well my Dad believed in them too. He would spend hours polishing his shoes, his shirts had to be immaculate and he never ever wore jeans or anything casual.

My Dad was kind in heart but it has to be said a little tight with his money and hid it under the bedroom carpet (except with us kids for Birthdays and Christmas when all the stops were pulled out)... he looked more than a little Italian and a bit like Robert De Niro (in reality our bloodline actually traces itself back to not Italian but Irish blood) and he was meticulous in his appearance. He was old fashioned and straight, hated to lose at cards and could nag the hind legs off a Buckinghamshire horse. I didn't know him for nearly long enough at all!

As well as my Uncle Nip for a brother, my Dad also had one sister- my Aunty Betty. She was a lovely kind woman. She looked like the actress Ingrid Bergman when she was younger and in later years, and being a little vain she took to wearing swinging sixties clothes. From behind she looked a right little Dolly bird, but when she turned round she showed her age. No-one criticised her for taking on the fashions of the time: it was just my Aunty Betty's way. Her husband was my Uncle George and he came from outside of Yorkshire (Cumbria to be exact) so there was always an element of he thought he was better than us Yorkshire Folk. Or maybe, to be fair, his hang ups may have been provoked by some provincial Yorkshire attitudes thrown upon him on admittance to the Beesley family! I don't know? My Mum said he was a suave type, too David Niven-like and a snob who thought he was better than us. He did look the part. I heard tales of him and my Dad almost at blows after drunken Christmas nights out. Tales of my Granddad wanting to play fisticuffs with anyone who wanted to partake were also told. One freezing cold and snowy Christmas he stripped down to his shorts and did the boxing shuffle, fists aloft ready for a fight after too much shandy and my Grandma, not a woman to be messed around with, shut him out in the snow until the morning to shouts of "C'mon come on out and show yer self I'll fight anyone of yer." No-one ever found out where he went that night and nothing was ever said about it again.

My Granddad was also a pit man. In fact my family tree reveals most of my ancestors to have worked in mining right back to the 1700's. Granddad was funny and old fashioned. I only knew him for a short time really. He gave me pennies to spend, laughed at me when acting out my impressions and had a look of Stan Laurel, complete with a short spiky tuft of hair and innocent expression. I was on our back garden one morning in 1971 when our Paul came with the news that Granddad had passed away.

Grandma was apparently a bit of a local legend around where they lived. She had her own special seat and table in the boozer across the road, the Fighting Cocks and she could drink most fellas under the table for a start. At the end of the war my Mum met her proper for the very first time at the Victory in Europe celebration party on Claypit lane. My Mum's recollections to me were of a big woman with a mass of black wavy hair flowing in the air as she danced around celebrating the end of the war. I don't think she even spoke to Mum that time and Mum was more than a bit wary of her. In time she grew to become close to her. I remember Grandma well. I too was a little scared of her. She had a fixed look that sent shivers down me. I used to visit her with my Mum over the years and later on, I would go and see her on my own to see if she needed anything. It would be deathly quiet in her house: the only sound would be the tick tock of the old clock on the cabinet. The cabinet was awash with ornaments of all types and sizes, with some of those old musical boxes. The room was dark and, to me, had an air of really old-fashioned (almost Victorian) days about it. I would sit there quiet- looking around, not knowing what to say. Five minutes may pass and then Grandma would say "Is our Ken alright Tony?" She was totally devoted to my dad. He could not take a wrong step in her eyes. I liked and cared for my Grandma... but, to be perfectly honest, I never felt one bit close to her.

I liked my Uncle George too; he was always kind and friendly with me. Years later when I was learning to play guitar he showed great interest in that and would tell me old stories of his younger days when he was learning to play drums for a jazz band. He also fancied himself as a singer too and would get up in the Fighting Cocks and sing old Cole Porter classics. Of course, helped along by copious amounts of strong pop I am told.

My Mum's sister was my Aunty Amy: I loved my Aunty Amy lots. She was funny, loved kids and never shut up talking! She was a live wire back in her school days and would always be getting chased all over Rawmarsh by the school bobby for not going to school. When her and my Mum went with the school for swimming lessons, the swimming teacher was belittling her so Amy pushed her into the pool, clothes n' all. Can't beat that!

As touched upon, the person that my Dad most loved to nag and row with was my Mother. My Mother was a proper Mum; she always put her kids first and never let us go without whenever she could help it. She was very kind, warm but also a bit stand-offish She would help anyone and was fiercely loyal to her family. Mild-tempered but if pushed could reveal a far deeper and darker side that would often surprise her foe: she was a true friend to anyone that got to know her and had a very self-deprecating sense of humour... as long as you didn't take it too far at her expense. My Mother adored kids and was young at heart through all of her 76 years; she loved Bingo, very rarely drank, chain-smoked till her fifties and, though not outwardly religious, believed in God. I knew her, cared for her and loved her and, like my dad, still dearly miss her!

Some early memories that I can vaguely recall are having my photo taken with one of those monkeys and my Dad at Scarborough around 1967, playing with my toy cars on the floor while 'Voyage to the Bottom of the Sea' was on the telly and naming one of my racing drivers Mick Jagger... also running around with a Thunderbirds hat on (what a pillock I must have looked... memories of it may have put me off going new romantic all those years later?) I remember asking my Dad where I came from and him, all unshaven, brushing his whiskery face against mine and saying "Well we found you under the apple tree and bought you for a pound of sugar." I also recall sat at the side of my brother, Glen watching a cowboy film and copying his every move - down to his every twitch and sniff, and from which came a common saying quoted from his reply to my method acting characterisation of his every movement. The saying (meaning *move up*) has been passed down to my kids to this day *"Budge up sniff."* The 1969 Moon landing was a big thing too. As we listened to this historical happening on the radio, my Dad and Mum openly stated that they didn't believe it was really happening saying it was all a fix and being taped in a studio... conspiracy theory number one!

As the 1960's approached their closing chapters, I settled down to a utopian existence of watching Dad's Army and cowboy films and playing with my toy soldiers. The heaps of Crescent, Lone Star and Britain's soldiers and cowboys and Indians (and the odd Tarzan and Batman figure) came pouring out of my toy box on a daily basis to provide a existence of adventurous paradise all re-enacted on the long battlefield of our furry jungle of a rug in front of the stove and coal fire. I would escape into my world of Wild West gunfights, Indian massacres, WW2 commando raids and Foreign Legion adventures: all set out in front of our Rediffusion black and white telly playing out episodes of 'The Virginian', 'Casey Jones', 'Captain Scarlet' and 'On the Buses.' Time stood still for a while: It was dead good!

....

I had seen a long trail of sad and distraught-looking kids passing by our front gate one afternoon while waiting for the Fletchers Bread and buns man to arrive (there were no supermarkets around back then and the local shops, being far and few between only opened certain hours). The closest thing to a supermarket was the local Coop: years later that turned into a VG store and got itself burned down... going on the out of date food it was selling, it's a wonder there wasn't some kind of prototype Chernobyl go off cos of the contamination of the food burning.

Our street back then was so quiet during weekdays: the Dads were all down the pit or at the Steelworks and the Mums were all probably doing the washing or something... unbelievably there was hardly any cars even then. There was an eerie calm, no police car sirens going off like nowadays when we seem to constantly live within a pretty hectic and never-ending episode of Starsky and Hutch. This would be around 1969... Anyway, these kids were passing by looking like they were retreating from the Russian front or something. My Mum told me that these pitiful figures were school kids: "leave 'em to it" I thought, "Nowt to do with me thank God!!!"

I was laid sprawled out on the rug with my regiments one afternoon, happy as a four year old kid could possibly be, when a knock on the door brought my world crashing down. I went to the door out of curiosity when I heard my name mentioned to my Mum who had answered the 'knock knock' demand. The woman at the door had sandy, mucky-blonde wavy hair. She was thin, big nosed, spotty and clearly had a cause. This woman was certainly not the classic sixties babe that history would have us believe was the norm. I mean this was still mid 1969 and our gritty northern world was still trying to fathom out exactly what the swinging, drug taking, mini-skirt wearing, Beatles-obsessed 1960's were really about. Our hippest scenesters were certainly hip to the Mod and post-Mod fashions of the day, but our average common household may have, by and large, not trodden that much further than 1963 Merseybeat. The woman at the door that day was nothing to do with any of this. Her mission was to discuss with my parents the sacrilegious idea of getting me a place in SCHOOL!

Ain't it weird, though how your early memories are all fuzzy and mixed up? It's like a proper 12 pence mix up of juggled memories that all merge into one with different tastes and sweet and bitter flavours: like the taste of fresh uncooked Brussels sprouts in me gob when our Paul says "Do yer want some spice Tone" (spice was our name for sweets), so like a pillock I excitedly says "Yes!" and after being told to shut me eyes and let him put one from the bag he has in my mouth ends up with a gammy mucky old sprout in me gob. Paul was in hysterics as I spat it out and went crackers at him. He was a swine our Paul and always up to some mischief. The teachers had told him he could go to University but he told them to get stuffed! We all think the world of him and he is one on his own.

Our Paul was 18 in 1965 when I was born; the perfect age to be in the mid 1960's just as everything was starting to happen. He was neither a Mod nor a Rocker – Ringo Starr may have appropriated his term of Mocker his way? – He saw the Beatles at the City Hall and thought they were crap and saw almost every other 'with it' band of the 60's either at the Mojo (where Peter Stringfellow allegedly banned him for a short while), the Esquire club (now the Leadmill) or the popular nights at Rawmarsh baths, where everyone from the Pretty Things, Soul legend Wilson Pickett, beat heart-throbs The Hollies, Tom Jones and a very young Lulu (who famously popped over to the Star pub across the road for a pre-performance drink) to Screaming Lord Sutch performed to packed out crowds of swinging beat fans, Mods, Rockers and everything in-between.

Our Glen, Grandma Beesley, Granddad Beesley, my
Uncle Mick and our Paul in 1965

Rawmarsh Baths was built in 1927 on the site of the old Rawmarsh Hall, which had been demolished earlier in the 20th century. The Baths were a gift from Earl Fitzwilliam to the residents of Rawmarsh and were used by generations of swimmers young and old, and also for the afore mentioned nights of entertainment as well as bouts of Wrestling events during the 1960's. Also commonly booked for wedding receptions and similar in the years since, the building was closed in 2001, closely followed by it being set alight and burnt beyond repair and consequent demolition. Influenced by the Rawmarsh Baths events and such was the fashion at the time, our Paul attempted to create his very own Beat group with some mates which they called 'Paul and the Daleks'. He acquired a Hofner bass just like Paul McCartney's which ended up being sold to fund a weekend at the coast when the band didn't make it big! Paul got married not long after in 1966.

Our Paul and Megan: late 1960's

The tail end of the sixties saw my two nephews Dave (born 1967) and Stephen (born 1968) join the Beesley clan. Our Paul and his new wife Megan got a house with them on Jackson Crescent sometime later. Being closer to my age than my own brothers, Dave and Steve became just like my own brothers in many ways. We were brought up together and were just as close as any brothers... we shared a lot of years and laughs together.

By this time, our Glen was about to leave school and start his long career as a joiner. Glen was eleven when I was born and used to look after me while me Dad were down the pit or the boozer and me Mum was at her beloved bingo. We used to watch cowboy films and wait for me Mum to return from the bingo with some prize-won Blue Riband biscuits or even better a massive box of snowballs. As soon as we heard her come in the door we would be upon her and if she had some we would grapple to get to them first and show how greedy we both could be. Glen was mad on football and Rotherham Utd and went all over to see 'em. His music of choice was Glam Rock when it filtered in during the early 70's and, like me, he also loved war films, particularly any aviation-themed ones. We went to see 'The Battle of Britain' at the old Odeon cinema when it came out in 1969. I can remember loving it, but being only just turned four years old I fell asleep for some of it. I awoke to see Herman Goering giving his pilots a dressing down for letting the Spitfires give 'em a pasting or two. Our Glen n' Paul also took me to see a re-run of 'Ben Hur' - we bought a programme for that one and I only slept for an hour and a half - and a bit later the newly-released 'Tora, Tora, Tora', 'Planet of the Apes' double bills (I stayed awake for all of those Monkey treats) as well as the Sean Connery Bond films, including my fave Bond movie 'Diamonds are Forever.' To see all those unbelievable stunts (believable to me at six years old) was amazing for me: watching Bond drive on two side wheels down a narrow alley got me clapping. And who were those two mysterious bad guy fellas, one being called Mr Kid? It's only when you watch the film years later that the penny drops that they were a pair of gay blokes. Sat munching on butterkist popcorn (which when I was asked do I want some butter-kiss, I had a vision in mind of some sloppy old codger coming along wanting to give me a kiss with a mouthful of butter, or worse still... Mr Kid.) Anyway, these cinematic delights, at such a young age, were a real treat.

Our Glen would excitedly scour through the Advertiser local paper for the listings on a Sunday dinnertime and if there was anything exciting showing we would be there. Thank God it wasn't all those sickly family themed films I was dragged along to, like the Sound of Music or something. Am I alone in wishing the Von Trapp family had gotten caught by the nasty Nazis on their escape journey through the Alps! No, my first cinema initiation was the sight of Spitfires and Hurricanes blasting Heinkels and Messerschmitts out of the sky over the cliffs of Dover and bloody damn good it was too! I have my two brothers, who I idolised, to thank for that!

In 1968-69, I was mad on Star Trek, which had just seen its very first UK TV airing (as well as Spock being the star of the front of the Sugar Smacks box). I can remember laid in bed and it taking me ages to count the crew of Star Trek from Kirk to Spock: All seven that I could remember. Through the influence of our Glen, my fave footie player was George Best, though I knew hardly owt about him, except that, to me, he looked just like a Beatle.

I can also remember the sounds of Lee Marvin singing 'Wandrin' Star' from our ancient transistor radio up on the window ledge and the hippy soundtrack 'If you go to San Francisco' (Wear some Flowers in your Hair) by Scott Mackenzie (released back in 1967): I thought the people who were singing these were actually in the little radio! Maybe they were? Hazy memories of our Glen having sneaky parties with mates and lasses round while Mum and Dad were out. I got sent to bed, being made to promise to not tell tales, but managed to persuade the Motherly instincts of the lasses to let me come down for a while and have a nosy. Other memories of sat at the table staring at the uniformed gas man counting the meter money out and stacking it up, thinking it was gonna be ours... NOT! We were so skint, sometimes and when he left us a whole £1 it was like Christmas all over. Talking of Christmas, I can just about remember the 1968 proper White Christmas, very hazy like, but I can still see that vision of looking through the front window at an endless blanket of snow. We had a false Snowman with a top hat on the inside and a real snowman with a fag in his gob outside, courtesy of our Paul!

I was well into all aspects of adventure and warfare even as a toddler starting off with shooting people with my plastic gun when going to the hospital to visit our Paul's wife, Megan, after she had our Dave. I had a bag of toy soldiers with me instead of a cuddly toy: I never had cuddly toys and showed no interest in typical little kid things. I was into war films, Westerns and anything with any fighting in: I would usually play with my soldiers while a film was on and say to whoever was in "Tell me when any fighting comes on." It was all a part of the generation we grew up with. Not many years before this a real war had been raging and its effect was still going on. My parents still had ragged old ration books in the drawer for Christ's sake!

Once, while the army were doing some recruiting in Rotherham town centre (outside the old Odeon cinema to be precise), I went up and asked the great big soldier in his smart uniform if I could join his army. Amazingly he said yes, just as soon as I was old enough. I was excited about that, but after a week of my imagination running away with my four year old mind, I decided to go and have another word on the following Saturday to tell him I may not be available for military service after all: I had visions of him dragging me away on the spot and taking me to my word of the week before. In truth he just smiled and patted me on the head. I still continued my obsession with all things military though, I just didn't want to join up and be told what to do and risk getting shot at!

My Aunty Betty and Uncle George used to run the Wellington pub in town and my Mum used to go and clean it for 'em for some extra pennies. She used to take me along, so that was how I was introduced to the small toy soldiers from Airfix, cos the big lads were too big to take many with us for me to play with while she did her work. The first boxes of Airfix HO/OO scale soldiers I had were British Commandos, then American Civil war Union infantry, Romans and WWI French Infantry... what a combination! So while we were there I would set these up and play out my imaginary battles... going careful to not disturb the resident cat!

They had a dog called Judy (soft as muck) and a black cat called Mr Tibbles (a psycho cat truth be known)... Mr Tibbles would give you a good whack with his paw as you passed: my Mother used to fight it with the cleaning brush; Mr Tibbles was a chicken-thieving- nasty piece of work, so you had to respect him. When my Aunty and Uncle left the pub the dog and cat were both put down, which we thought was really sad.

Back on to the soldiers obsession, while we were at the Wellington pub (a very earthy styled pub... my Uncle Mick, their son, was a very abiding patron too)... my Mother would occasionally take me up the winding stairs up to the special room that was always locked up and inside it were lots of red bandsmen's uniforms... just like those Goldstream guards that Airfix had out. Mum would sneakily unlock the room and let me have a peek at it all. I loved that and it was a special treat. Life was a bit of a treat to be honest, nothing to complain about at all. All in all, everything was great and I was having a good time! Then everything changed when that visit earlier by the school woman came up with an official result: me going to chuffing' school! And so begins the true beginning of this story: My school years to come - of 1969 to 1976, when some my life's most hilarious, innocently mischievous and colourful days would occur on my bike journey through the 1970's to Punk Rock!

Chapter Two

A pair of Red Flares

"It was an absolute joke! I was all of five years old and on my way to school and getting laughed at good and proper, and why was this display of merriment going on? It was cos I was wearing a pair of bright-red Hippy-flared loon pants. It was windy that day and the flares were flapping all over the place and the gusts of wind were flowing up each leg and ballooning the trousers out... what a clown!"

A cousin from Bradford's 1970's flared trouser-endorsing Club double act

1969: my first day at school! Rawmarsh infants' school was the destination for my initiation into the world of early Education. I arrived, along with a whole platoon of gob-opened-wide anxious kids, hanging on to their Mums' apron strings, for a whole full day of schooling with no idea that this was gonna be a regular habit. Unfortunately, no one told me this would be permanent. *"OK I can handle one day only"...* I was trying to kid myself on. It worked for a short while.

29

We were left in the hands of our mature and knowledgeable infant's school teacher for our first day's schooling. All was quiet for a few minutes; then the screaming started! Kids were crawling all over the place, some trying to hide, others making a well aimed on all fours gallop for the gateway to freedom of the classroom door. Some were trying to impress with their best renditions of 'kid in an electric chair' all octopus-like arms flailing and manoeuvring with extreme vigour. Not to be really noticed, and this may have been a legend spread by some nervously exhausted infant teacher, but there may have been just one or two kids holding their own and keeping their nerve in the true spirit of Dunkirk. Me? I was slowly being smothered in warm and tender Motherly reassurance in the arms of a girl called Vanessa. My tears of separation from my regiments and legions of 32mm paint shedding plastic soldiers were being slowly eased away in a slumber of female security. *"School can't be all that bad"* was the train of thought as 10am moved into 11am. That was until the spectre of lunchtime appeared. I had no idea that I would have to be retraining my eating habits into co-habiting with a 100 multi-coloured sweater-wearing, candle snot-balancing horde of hungry or too upset to eat fellow kid prisoners. I could well have invented eating disorders that day: I certainly had the early training to set me on that path!

All that morning, the prospect had never entered my head. We were ushered into the school hall at lunchtime and mustered into some sort of order (*"You sit there sweetheart next to him, he has a similar colour jumper on"*) and then expected to consume that pink 'cat food smelling' piece of shoe leather that was sat looking lonely but unsociably inedible on our shiny white plates. My decision was made spontaneously. No way on earth was I gonna sink my much loved milk teeth into that excuse for a school lunch. C'mon Dinner ladies and school authoritarian headmistress in person, bring on your best, but I am gonna sit this one out. No compromise. This is my decision. You want it? You have it! Me no want it, me no have it!

The Dinner lady was a lovely woman but the lunch-munching mission simply failed when applied to my attention. I turned my back to teacher and dinner lady in protest and went hungry, happy in the thought that I had won my first battle, if not campaign, away from headquarters, and looked forward to going home and reviewing the troops.

I got home that night experiencing a new kind of tiredness. One I had not experienced before, but undoubtedly would be re-introduced to again and again over the years. My first day of school over, I forgot to report to Fort Timpo that evening. Instead, I got on the settee before our Glen came home and settled down to a nice good old fashioned nap. Blimey! It had been a long hard day. My days of freedom were now over!

My infant's school band audition

The famous swinging sixties were also now over. The Hippy dream supposedly ended with the Rolling Stones concert at Altamont Speedway track (USA) on December 6th 1969 when all notions of free love, peace and loving thy fellow man and woman (as regularly as possible it is said) were shattered with an attack of Hell's Angels-inflicted violence. Woodstock had been and gone (August 1969), long hair went mainstream and the revolution was apparently over. And, those loveable Mop tops the Beatles who were by now bearded long-haired Jesus look-alikes with political and spiritual agendas; were no longer friends with each other and would soon part their ways. For me, though, the sixties dream (whatever that was) had ended with that first day at school!

So school had begun... worse luck. The Infants school years consisted of being banged on the head at each side with two crates of milk bottles in the grasp of the caretaker, being taught that Peter and Jane were clever little kids and maybe one day we could be like them, Mary was a virgin, train drivers weren't all called Casey Jones and all the while inhaling old fashioned teachers' bad breath and their stupefied ideas of what the big world was all about... fun it was not! The only bit of early Infants school-time fun was had from throwing the newly available (1969) stickle bricks at kid's jumpers to which they would stick very well. We had no real choice at not attending school so I may as well have some fun. I began to associate kids with the colour of their school jumper – freshly created by knitting-mad Mothers. If Simon wore a green jumper, he is remembered as green and likes horrible Marrowfat peas and picks green bogeys and eats 'em. If Alan had a yellow jumper then he likes bananas and singing 'Yellow Bird in a Banana tree'... Perfect!! My contribution to the fashion of the time was not by choice either. I got bought the just-mentioned pair of bright-red Hippy-styled Loon pants... bell bottoms or whatever you wanna call them. I hated the sight of them especially when I wore them to school and halfway down the street, all of the kids was laughing their heads off at 'em... and I don't blame them either. Not surprisingly, I never wore them ever again!

Relief from my one and only ordeal of school lunch-time torture and its extended misery of continuous schooling came from the obligatory Saturday trip to town for the traditional 25p pocket money spend. Back then, for 25 pence exactly; I could get a brand new Matchbox car and either a box of Airfix soldiers or a selection of Timpo soldiers or cowboys and Indians. The location for these was the old Rotherham Market, of which I can just about remember, clearly enough to see, in my mind's eye now: the beehive hair dos of the fag-in-gob bargain-hunting Mums, kids dragged by the Ajax-scoured hands around the packed aisles and inviting stalls... the most inviting of all for me being the good old toy stall.

I used to love a good old rummage through the open boxes of Timpo figures at the front of the toy stall, choosing either a Roman centurion, Crusader, US Cavalry man or British infantry with back packs and removable berets: well everything on a Timpo figure was removable, just about. It wouldn't take them long to be in the toy box collection, back at home and not so long before each figure could end up being a unique mix up of a warrior. Ever seen a Medieval Knight with a flame thrower and a back pack of grenades on hand for support? That old Rotherham market was chocca-block full of shoppers, all searching and milling around for the full weeks shop and bargains to boot. Then one day it got demolished!

The other main toy outlet was Woolworths, where I once nutted the glass food cabinet in a fit of temper when getting bored of all the Saturday morning shopping and being over-eager to get to the toy section. Well, I had to spend my 25p didn't I? Woolworths did typical High Street toys and Airfix, but not as extensively as that last bastion of Toy solidarity and kids toy heaven- Coopers Toys on Doncaster gate!

Inside the old Rotherham Market where I spent many a Saturday scavenging for toys: a new block of flats stands on the spot now (Photo courtesy of Tim Jones)

Coopers toy shop was opened as a family business way back and was the greatest toy shop ever!!! Christ how would you start to describe Coopers toys? It was a kid's paradise. It had everything a kid could want. Kids of all ages could be satisfied by what it had to offer. The store was actually two departments; it had a downstairs shop with all the board games (stacked to toy oblivion in the lead up to Christmas) and a gob-smacking selection of every kids annual you could ever imagine all shelved up neatly - spine showing - from each September to Christmas. The rest of the year it stocked less interesting stuff in that section, but don't ask me what? A trip up the stairs of that lower section and a turn to the left and you were in the Model world of Airfix. Now this section was immense. It was layered wall to wall with everything that Airfix and any other reasonable model making companies had to offer at the time. Models of all scales, sizes and affliction lined the vast never-ending walls and at each section there would be spinners with Airfix HO/OO scale soldiers: everything from Robin Hood and his merry men and the best of the French Foreign Legion to World War two Japanese Infantry and their opponents the US Marines. Exactly what I have come for then!! Those small boxes of soldiers and the forts and play sets were my favourites of all. I loved the colourful artists' impressions of warfare slapped all over the front of the boxes and when I got them home, I would rip the figures off their sprues and set them up on the carpet exactly as the front of the box showed, or as close as I could get anyhow.

Leaving the world of Airfix behind and continue across the exit way, a peek up to the left in Coopers saw a steep set of stairs that at Christmas would host that red-suited merry maker Father Xmas himself up there (probably some old git that hated kids if truth be known). Down the stairs, which if I recall rightly were solid stone, and the next department was awaiting downstairs. This section was like a separate shop and you could also enter it from the outside and by-pass the shop below on the street. Hosting everything from Britain's figures (Swoppets, plastics and from 1971 the classic Detail range with their metal stands), jigsaws, the girls stuff (boring), the latest toy gadgets (Viewfinders, chemistry sets etc) Lego (including their annual Lego competition) and kids bikes WOW!!! So many hours were spent in that shop and when I think back to it, it brings back nothing more than happy smiling memories. When that shop closed down in the 1990's I was never the same!! A part of my childhood had been cruelly taken away; I had had visions of buying toys there with my grandkids in later years. Cheers for that Meadowhell!

1970 sounded brand new, no more 1960's, this decade would be futuristic and by the end of it we would be riding around in space-styled automobiles in the air above our cosmic super modernised cities, just like it was depicted in those old Valiant and Lion comics and Eagle annuals. This was the modern world. This was the future.

That first year of this new 70's utopia, of which I can recall a good bit of, started off with The Who's iconic Live at Leeds being recorded and released, Mick Jagger being fined £200 for possession of cannabis, the first real Heavy Metal album being released courtesy of Black Sabbath, the Concorde making its first supersonic flight at 700 mph, the U.S invading (and later withdrawing from) Cambodia, the Beatles officially disbanding around the time of their last (official) studio album 'Let it Be', Brazil beating Italy 4-1 in the World Cup Final and Jimi Hendrix dying as Elvis Presley returned to the stage. Back at my neck of the woods, I was more pre-occupied in getting through my early formative years at school and, to begin with, it all seemed like one long endless drag!

My new teacher in the 2nd year was useless and I learned absolutely nothing from her. I couldn't hear or understand her as the days went by and I just fell behind more and more with my schoolwork, to the point I was behind almost all of the rest of the class. Consequently I missed out on learning my alphabet, basic numbers, general reading and writing and whatever else this 1940's throwback teacher was trying to teach us! It took some time before I caught up and even then, my attention span was very limited, especially where it concerned anything I wasn't interested in. It was gonna be a very long haul to get through my next twelve years or so of schooling.

In 1971, the old Market that I had only really just got to know and love closed down to make way for a new one at the other side of town. I can remember the first time I went to the new market, keenly looking out for any prospective stalls of interest. As it happens, to quote that long-haired-cigar-smoking-warbling DJ, Jimmy Savile, this new market was great too, with plenty of things of interest for me to be found. For a start Coopers' toys also had a stall there. Then, there was the used books and comics stall, where I would buy and swap bags of Commando books over the years and scavenge over someone's old Hotspur comic collection now priced at a new penny each or 15 for 10 pence. The outside market also had stuff of interest too, so things weren't all so bad. Something had to spoil my first little trip to Market? The Market quickly became a busy, bustling place. Passing by the crowds of trolly-pulling housewives and fellow nagging kids, I came face to face with an old woman with a sunken in eye. She had a dark-tanned complexion, lots of wrinkles and was thin as a skeleton... but it was that sunken eye that got my attention. It scared me and I couldn't get the vision out of my head of 'the incredible sunken eye woman' in Rotherham Market. It was my Saturday afternoon appointment with fear!

The new Rotherham Market area 1970's

My kid imagination often took me to places other kids never went and it's a good job there was plenty of good toys and games around to keep it at hand. Make no bones about it, Toys were exciting back then. They were colourful antidotes to the real world. They ranged from Chemistry sets (don't think I ever had one of them, though, but me and our Steve did try and make our own salted peanuts once, with a bag of monkey nuts and some lard in a pan that nearly set the house afire, does that count as a chemistry set?)... there were Die-cast toys, Tonkas, the newly produced Action Man - of whom I had the Red Devil, but never really warmed to him so got him shot - Meccano (a bit hard to use, but intriguing all the same), the immortal Lego (one toy that has survived to this day, which is more than I can say about all those attempts at building battleships to float in the bath with it). Then there were various stuff based on the popular action-based TV shows of the day - The Avengers, Batman, Man from Uncle, UFO, Space 1999 and Thunderbirds etc, all being future collecatbles.

Speaking of the telly it wasn't on nowhere near as much back then. For a start there were only two and a half channels anyway: Yorkshire Television (and its associated companies) the dependable BBC1 and then BBC2, which we managed to get around 1970. When we did manage to tune into it, the channel was only on for a few hours and was mostly stuff that went straight over our heads... well mine at least. The TV would start around lunch time, except for some schools education programmes in the morning slots, and would end with a midnight all clear with the National anthem on BBC1.

Infants school ID parade... arrows pointing to me, Mark Barnet (future Punk Rocker Barney Rubble) and at the bottom my mate Julian Jones

In-between that, was a mix of plays, weekend game shows ('The Golden Shot' with Bob Monkhouse and Brucie in 'the Generation Game'), 'Opportunity Knocks' (My dad's pet hate- Hughie Green, who as much as he hated the man, he still insisted we all watch him and his show so we could all listen to him pull him to pieces)... the ever-green but perpetually gloomy and very black n' white scary Ena Sharples-starring 'Coronation Street', some kids shows like 'Play Away', 'Clangers' the enthralling 'Mr Ben' and the like early on and a host of TV series that became almost as much a part of living as waking up in a morning... 'This Is Your Life' (that theme tune could send me back to the early 70's on a single hearing as does any mention of 'Whicker's World', 'World in Action' and 'Panorama!') But they were adult and their fusty yawn-inducing appeal escaped my world of imagined war and adventure. I wanted action, fun and explosions!

The TV Shows that got my attention were 'Dads Army', 'Doctor Who', 'The Fenn Street Gang', 'On the Buses' (I loved Reg Varney and his pal Jack and their antics), 'Hogan's Heroes' and all of the Western series such as 'Bonanza', 'Wagon Train' (its repeats coming to an end just in time for me to catch them and mimic the characters for a laugh - gid ey up gid ey up!!!), 'The Virginian' and then a bit later on 'The High Chaparral' and

'Alias Smith and Jones.' The Kids' TV shows were something special, though not all to my taste. 'Magpie' (presented by 'Scars of Dracula' star Jenny Hanley, poodle-haired Mick Robertson and Douglas Rae) and 'Take Hart', 'Pipkins', 'Mr Trimble' (the theme tune to which we would hum as we went to school along with 'The Pink Panther Show'), Ron Ely in 'Tarzan', the immortal Dick Dastardly and Mutley and co and their hilarious antics in 'Whacky Races' and its spin off 'Catch the Pigeon', 'Scooby Doo' a chuckle at Parrot Face and many others: all possibly capturing those final few years when Kids were still wide-eyed and in awe of adventure, colour and being as daft as Basil Brush. The enemies were 'Follyfoot', 'Black Beauty', The Partridge Family' and 'Upstairs Downstairs.' And who can forget that grinning lass that never stopped eye-balling yer on the BBC when nowt was on? Wonder what she looks like now? Oh and what about the Smash advert? That was some technical advance at the time that was, talking tin men that could miraculously plug Cadbury's Smash too. I couldn't work out how a chocolate brand could make mashed potatoes: would they taste of their best chocolate bars, was that their appeal? Anyway I preferred 'Charlie says' ads to be honest 'Charlie says meeeee, rrrrrrr, grrrrrr, meeeee!'

'Here come the Double Deckers' (1971) was the true sign that the weekend was here for us young 'uns. It was a programme that made me wanna go out and join the kids in the programme and live out their world of kids' espionage and antics. I never did ever manage to acquire a hide-out as cool as a Double Decker bus hidden in a secret yard, though. That programme, along with 'It's 5 'O Clock and its Crackerjack' was the starting grid! I still worship Fridays and I think my adulation of the day may have its roots in these programmes and the knowledge that school could be forgotten about for a whole two and a half days.

Other weekend TV treats would be that crazy games inventions show 'It's a Knockout' lots of fun and if you didn't end up laughing along with it, you must have been dead. That and the generational kid fave Doctor Who. I can vaguely remember the last episodes of the Patrick Troughton years, but my fave Doctor was Jon Pertwee. Like Sean Connery is the iconic James Bond, then Jon Pertwee is Doctor Who. I got hooked on Doctor Who through the Pertwee years; it was part of the Saturday TV staple diet. The Daleks were still rampant (I even got to meet a real Dalek at a Dr Who exhibition in

Blackpool one year) and the British army were in support for the doctor in defeating countless scary creatures- in effect merely blokes in fancy suits with messed up masks. It was fun, exciting and addictive. When Tom Baker arrived, he became a new generation of Dr Who fans' own favourite Doctor, well my enthusiasm waned and I moved onto something else.

The only downside to weekends, then and now, is the comedown as Monday morning looms and glooms like a vulture out to eat your very being and sense of happiness. When I was a kid, it started on a Sunday... usually late afternoon when my Mum was ignoring me for being unruly or giving her, or someone else, some cheek. She knew I couldn't stand being ignored. By Sunday night as bath time had arrived, the rot had firmly set in.

For some unknown reason (when she had gotten round to talking to me) as if to try and cheer me up in some way, my Mum would always blow-dry my hair into an Elvis style and show me my pissed off mug through the little round mirror from the bath room, saying "There Tony, you look just like Elvis now." I didn't feel like a multi-millionaire Rock n Roll singer on a Sunday night, I can tell yer and I am sure I looked nowt like a six year old Elvis either!!! As the gloom of Monday morning, and that rotten institution (School) became more of a distinct and serious threat, the only consolation was to wait until the claustrophobic Victorian cruise brochure 'The Onedin Line' was done with (another allergy-inducing telly programme... haaaaa!) and watch the Sunday night movie with Charlton Heston in (or Charles Heston as my Mother called him)... it was usually 'Major Dundee', 'The Warlord', 'The Big Country' or '55 Days at Peking' and Charles er Charlton Heston was in 'em all! And if it were not for the sound of my Victor comic dropping through the letter box around 8.15am the next day, even Charlton Heston would not have dragged me out of bed for bloody School!

Speaking of Charles, my Mum always got the names of people and things wrong and mixed up, causing countless moments of hilarity for me. I can still remember when she would browse the TV guide in the Daily Express (remember back then we didn't know what was on the telly till the actual day) and she would come out with allsorts of re-arranged film titles. Try these for size - "Jason and the Astronauts is on this afternoon Tony"... and "Bloomin' eck that film is on again Fizzo" ('Psycho' she meant).There were plenty more too, long consigned to my forgotten memory box.

Meanwhile back at school, I was coming towards the end of my stay at the Infants school and it had been a weird experience: a sort of introduction to what we were expected to be moulded into for our future adult life. It was ok at times – in small doses, I suppose – and on the positive side, I had made some great new mates... big Bry Haller, Nicky Booth, Pete Roddis and others, along with my two best pals Andy and Gary... but, I was, even at that early age, showing signs of not wanting to fit in with the general scheme of things. I was starting to develop a dislike of some teachers and especially the head-crushing caretaker and often would have to be really persuaded that I had to go to school: often hiding away in the upstairs cupboard or outside toilet. I can imagine my parents would have been maybe thinking "Oh no, not a repeat of our Paul." Pretty soon, the move over to the nearby Junior school would be here. Perhaps, that would be more fun than this Peter and Jane induction centre!

In 1971, I saw the first dead person I had ever seen! It was a Saturday morning and I had gone to Rotherham town centre with me Mum to spend my 25p spending money in Cooper's toy shop, hoping to get back in time to watch Dickie Davies reel off what was coming up on 'World of Sport' and then watch the Wrestling with me Dad later on, all after an hour or two playing with a new box of Airfix soldiers. As we walked up past bustling crowds of un-pedestrianised Bridgegate past Wilson Pecks, I spotted a gathering of people and an Ambulance. Walking past the crowd of people that were all gazing down towards the floor, I was told by my Mum to not look at what they were looking at. My childish curiosity got the better of me and as I peered through the people stood there, I saw, laid on the floor all hunched up, a man motionless and a coat of crimson seeping all around his grey haired head. "Is he dead." I asked Mum. "I told you not to look, Tony." Mum replied grabbing my hand and dragging us away and out of sight of the accident. I don't know what happened next... if the man really was dead or if he was just unconscious, but he was not moving and seemed to be not breathing either and the look on people's faces was not good. I pestered Mum to tell me and she concluded that she thought that he was probably dead, but he wouldn't have been in any pain. It appeared that he had been run over by a bus. I remembered that poor bloke for some time. I also, remember thinking that maybe life was not always fair and people can get hurt much more easier than I had previously imagined. For now, though, I tried to put it out of my mind and my biggest worry was to get to the Cherryade pop first when the Alpine blokes delivered it next Friday.

1971 was the year of Space Hoppers and UK Decimalisation. Arsenal beat Liverpool in the F.A cup at 2-1, Jim Morrison of The Doors was found dead in a bath-tub in Paris, British troop presence in Northern Ireland increased and on New Years Eve American actor Pete Duel of 'Alias Smith and Jones' Western TV series tragically committed suicide.

In 1971 our Glen bought a reel to reel tape recorder, which was kind of state of the art (at least to us anyway) for the time. We had some great fun with that. Stevie from next door used to come round on a Saturday night and have us all in stitches with his impersonations of celebrities, which we would record on the tape machine. We managed to record Dad moaning, our Paul singing 'Jesus Christ Superstar', me acting the fool, our classic arguments and the Top Ten tunes on a Sunday tea-time from the radio as well as the theme tune and opening intro to 'Alias Smith and Jones'. It was a great laugh and a big novelty. I wish we still had those tapes to listen to once more and bring 1971 back to life again.

Also in 1971, our Paul and Megan had their third (and last) child- our Michelle. I can remember not being told what was going on, as if to try and kid me on that babies still came from under the apple tree or something! One minute, late on in the pregnancy, I was told something along the lines of "There is going to be a new baby coming soon"... oh really, and then the next minute (as if by post), our Michelle was here. I can still remember the very first time I saw her. I was up at their house and Megan was holding her and I asked to hold her too. Our Michelle was my new niece... I had not had one of those before: Little did I know that I was being pruned for a baby sitting job in a few years down the line. That would be a precarious invite, on our Paul and Megan's part: they only found out in later years about all the broken ornaments and larking around we all got up to as soon as they had gone around the corner at the bottom of the street, but more of that later.

For the time being, our Michelle was a quiet little baby, we were all a close family apart from the odd scrap and blazing row which was our tradition every now and again, usually nearing the end of the Christmas period. We didn't know it at the time, but thinking back, I bet the neighbours could almost time the moment that the Beesleys would kick off again... usually to the sounds of plates being smashed and the bump of our Glen getting thumped off our Paul cos he got more chips than him or something! We had to release our tension somehow, and for a good ten to fifteen years we fought, fell out and disagreed as often as an argument was available. The Beesleys could sometimes not like each other, but let anyone else say so and we wouldn't be having none of it!

Mum and our little Michelle

Times could be tough sometimes. But my Mother and Dad held things together as much as they could. Dad even tried fixing the telly, the over-sized 'Churchilean' Radio and our clocks, but very rarely ever succeeded: my Mum always said electrical items needed time to wear in, much to our impatient responses. My clothes were mostly home-knitted (except Whitsuntide, when for some unknown reason we had a new set of clothes bought) and we had no heating in the house except for a living room coal fire – lovely for toasting and roasting chestnuts: but we managed to be (mostly) happy! We only got our first fridge in 1973 and a colour telly four years later. Besides my Dad believed that freezing food was bad for you and half of his favourites on the telly were black and white. Our oven was above the fireplace, the washing got done once a week on a Tuesday in the old-fashioned twin tub... us kids drunk water straight out of the tap, ate sweaty cheese with mucky hands and fast food was watching our Paul demolishing a chip butty. We hardly had any money or owt posh but we all mucked in together, fall outs n' all. Besides, we had holidays to look forward to together!

Kid on a Red Chopper Bike - Tony Beesley

Chapter Three

Holidays in the Sun!

"Those day-trips to the seaside! The journey on the coach there would involve sights of travel-sick kids looking as green as the Incredible Hulk, fag smoke drifting from all directions of the bus, games of Snap, Dandelion and Burdock pop being guzzled down (and back up again) and always a bloke with a bald head who looked like Olive's hubby off 'On the Buses' dishing out crisp, instructions and sandwiches."

Back in the late 1960's and throughout the best part of the 70's, it was virtually unheard of to hear of anyone taking holidays abroad. Christ, we were thankful for our weeks at Costa del Brid, Port de Skeggy, Flamingo land, Castleton and on a couple of occasions when my Dad might have felt a little flush, a week (or maybe) a fortnight at the cream of the Norfolk coast; Great Yarmouth.

Our typical 70's family seaside fun, Mother in required fashion item of the time – the housewives' scarf

These exciting and fiercely enticing sun-drenched (or just drenched) forays to the coast for a week of beach-hugging, arcade-obsessed, crab-hunting mayhem were supported by a series of what seemed like regular daytrips with all of the working men's clubs within drinking distance of my Dad and my eldest brother.

On these daytrips, us kids pocketed our genuine one pound note spending money, scoffed the free bags of XL crisps on the bus and travelled by cream coaches with different colour stripes down the side to Scarborough, Bridlington, Skegness, Cleethorpes, Morecambe and Blackpool, eager and hopeful to be able to manage to spread our spending money on a spree of ice cream, penny arcade mania, rock, donkey rides, donuts, candyfloss, a bucket and spade set with flags and enough left to take a toy back home for a souvenir. If not, there would be plenty of pleas, bribery and stubborn protests to our nagging Mums – who by the end of the day would be starting to wonder if the blokes would be back in time from the boozer to catch the coach home. Sounds like chaos and strife? Nah it was just part of the fun and experiences of a family daytrip or the bigger relative: a real full week's holiday to the seaside.

One trip to Skegness saw me and our Dave n' Steve go crab-hunting under the pier while the tide was out. The grown ups were up the beach, demolishing the sarnies, fags and cockles and mussels while we had a bit of fun. The fun soon turned to slight concern when we realised that we had been surrounded by the incoming tide. The temptation to leave us where we were must have been overwhelming but we were rescued by the Life-guard services... of our Paul and Megan's brother Pat – on their shoulders.

Now, I have no idea why we were there, but I can also recall us ending up at Grimsby docks on one occasion. All I can remember is me and our Glen getting lost and trying to find a way back to the others. Anyway, this foreign sailor appeared out of nowhere (maybe he was a Nazi prisoner who had fell off a boat in the docks after years of being trapped down below?) So as we were going up and down these Grimsby back alleys and looking for a way out of this Fisherman's maze, this sailor, first asked us something in his language, and then wouldn't stop following us: he probably thought that we knew where we were going, but we didn't. Our Glen wasn't the nasty type, but after being stalked for, what seemed like ages, he started to lose his patience. I was saying "Are yer gonna smack him, Glen, go on belt him!!" I really think he would have belted him one, but, as we turned around a corner onto a street with a chippy on, we bumped straight into our Paul, who takes one look at Hans Gruberstein who on seeing our Paul's inhospitable chip-munching frown, takes one turn around and scarpers like hell back around the corner. And that was the end of the Grimsby Docks chase!

There was a proper holiday to Great Yarmouth whilst I was really still quite young, but I can't remember much, if anything about that one. Likewise a late 60's week at Scarborough, of which I can only vaguely remember setting off in an old grey Morris Minor car and breaking down on the way. Somehow, I seem to recall it being misty, though that could be my memory or my bed sheet-filled eyes at the time.

The first holiday in decent memory was a week at Skegness in 1971. We hired a caravan with no heating, the obligatory toilet block at the other side of the camp and fold out seating for beds. It was a family holiday (with some family members missing) and while my Dad and Glen got right excited and went up in a three seater aeroplane, me and my four year old nephew 'Diddy' Dave were both being gits! Our first venture involved him sweeping up some dry dog shit with his spade and placing it strategically at the bottom of the play slide whilst some kids we had been falling out with came zooming excitedly down the narrow slippery slope straight into it. They were bigger than us and one of the lads was around 12 and his response to our dirty deed was to shout a word at us that I had never heard before in my life. He was chewing on Toffoe's and blurted out a sentence that contained a brand new word - a totally new to my ears discovery - the word was 'F***in'. When I went back to the grown ups later on I couldn't wait to ask what this new 'F***ing' word meant exactly! My Mum's face was a picture.

The dog shit mission was part of a series of holiday misdeeds and sneaky naughtiness we performed while the grown ups were distracted by booze, bingo, fake seafront auctions and re-enacting the adventures of Biggles in the Skegness sky. We returned from good old Skeggy with sunburn, grazes, sugar-coated teeth and sun-kissed classic 1970's slightly longer hair. Speaking of seafront auctions - none ever concluded quite as funny as the one our Paul dragged us all along to on Blackpool front one year. He was always after a bargain and never could resist the luring temptation of these *Northern Del boys in the making* - broadcasting their amazing deals through a bass heavy microphone in a 'rent for a day' open planned store. One of these confidence tricksters managed to convince him that the gigantic oversized box of Dairy Milk chocolates were the bargain of the day. He bid and bid and won the shrink-wrapped selection of Cadburys finest and, satisfied the winning price was a snatch then proceeded to taunt us all. We thought we were all in for a treat but the treat we did get was one of side-splitting laughter for us all when Paul eventually opened his box of goodies to savour some sweet-toothed pleasure at our mouth watering expense. The oversized box of succulent best brand chocolates was - an empty box! A good few more coast-visiting treats came our way during the next few years... a time of sand castle-building rivalry; 'Kiss me Quick' hats, aniseed rock-chomping, saucy postcard naughtiness and plenty of fun for all!

Bridlington 1973 started out as a fantastic holiday. I had performed my last pre-holiday duties with my toy soldiers the previous day; a sunny excitable Friday afternoon in the middle of the six weeks holidays. That night, I could hardly sleep. The images of never ending days on the beach and playing in the frothy sea amongst many more 'can't wait for moments' kept me from sleeping hardly one bit that night. I couldn't wait!

We hired a holiday camp chalet this time - Hi-De-Hi! style without Paul Shane... just our Paul. This was a full membership family holiday. Headed by my Dad in his ever present black suit, crisp white shirt and spotless shoes and tie and the formidable serious 'Mums know best' approach of my Mum and Megan; what could go wrong? We had our Paul on hand for jokes and unplanned mayhem, Glen for history of aviation knowledge and a small varied assortment of kids; me, our Dave, Steve and our little Michelle. We must have come across as some mix of 'On the buses meets the Likely Lads with the Double Deckers' and the Fenn Street gang' in support.

That summer holiday was great: The parts of it that actually happened that is, which were like a magical place to be... kid's adventure heaven. I remember late nights playing adventurous army manoeuvres scaling the grassy 'cliff-like bluffs' at the end of the camp site, re-enacting the D-Day invasion. Somehow me and the lads got to stop out later than usual. We would arrive back at the chalet quite late on... red hot, sweaty and filthy with no caps left in our silver pistols and gagging for a swig of Tizer. We had a great go on a Tarzan-parachute swing style of a ride up near Flamborough Head. We got to do lots of exciting, adventurous and funny things. Late nights too, of our Paul taking me, Dave and Steve on the Waltzer and Speedway when it was speeded up for the last hour. Pissed up he would drag us on and we would hang on with the skin of our teeth as we went whizzing around. It felt like paradise for a short while, and the fun would never end. Half way through the holiday, us being crammed two to a bed, lights went out late one night and throughout the night I scratched and scratched. The morning came and whilst my Mother was making breakfast and the fellas had gone out for an early morning stroll for a paper and fags, my tired eyes opened to a new sunny day. As I started to get out of bed, I saw a little black thing crawling across the bed. It also had a mate on the march not far behind. *"Hey up Mother, what are these little black creepers I can see in here?"* I shouted through. My Mother came through, took one look at the creatures, and then took another look around the room. Her eyes were startled and alert as she lifted the bed sheets up. The little creeper patrol had a whole regiment marching not far behind. She checked out the other beds. Dad arrived back in. The grown ups were alerted and put on stand by. *"Looks like the chalet has got bugs."* was the conclusion. Bang goes the holiday now!

Our Paul, my Dad and the other grown ups put up a right case when they got the owners in to inspect. The commotion was not half as bad as the one me and the kids put up when we found out the holiday was done and finished. We had only just got into the action... No, surely not. It can't be?

Anyway, the grown ups did their stuff. The blokes got some money back for our troubles and us kids were promised a replacement holiday as soon as we got home. Umm? Was that really gonna happen then? We packed up and crammed into a return mini-bus bound for home. Then it started to piss it down with rain. Our faces were direly miserable. It was downright depressing. What an end to our holiday. We were told by our parents not to mention the Bug hut (as we had now christened it). My Dad was a very proud fella. My Mum was allergic to shame and I suppose our world of Attenborough escapade was not really something to brag off about.

Consequently we were told not to tell anybody about the bugs no matter what. I mean what would our mates say? We already had a fair roster of cruel nick names for less house-proud family's kids, so no way were us mostly clean-living citizens going to get tarred with their mucky brushes. Nowadays the stigma has been shed. Infact, a modern contemporary family would collect a 'quids in' court case against the company these days. Us, we were quite happy to try and put the whole thing behind us. Now where was that replacement holiday then?

....

The replacement holiday never came that year. Instead, we were treat to a series of Sunday afternoon car rides in our Glen's Hillman Avenger to Castleton, around eight of us crammed in there, hot, sweaty and impatient and wondering if the delights of the underground caves and sights of our destination would be worth the endless traffic jams and wrong turns it took to get there. Sure, there were other exciting things going on for the 70's generation of restless, thrill-seeking young un's of our end during the annual six weeks school holidays. Apart from table football and head-dodging games of Darts on the back garden, there was always a game of good old footie on the school field: this being in the days before schools became more representative of military prisons with their security systems, spiked railing fortifications and ex SAS caretakers and you could have a good game of 'jumpers for goal-posts' and 'play till the football busts' footie within the closed school grounds. Generally you received no real hassle from the caretakers (and believe me Mr Hitler would have taken no restraint from belting us given half the chance) unless things got out of hand. That is unless you decided to practise the local junior golf championship and put the main classroom big window through with a golf ball like our Steve did one year: he was mortified, we were in stitches!
So football was an option and one taken up by most of the local lads for at least a good proportion of the holidays. Some damned good red-hot and sweat-drenched days flew by while participating in the local football leagues that were put together about as democratically as Hitler's rise to power in 1933. The idea of a fair and well-balanced football side with the ace players

divided equally never seemed to happen, and you would most likely end up playing a full days footie with your fellow useless Peter Bonnetti and Billy Bremner wannabes against a side of seasoned full-kitted lads that would endlessly score goals as I was waving at someone on the bus I knew; ultimately being left with a thigh full of stud prints for proof of our defeat.

Personally, I never took football that seriously. There were always a gang of the lads who would be obsessed with everything related to the game and knew every player, manager and ground off by heart. My interest went as far as the actual attempting to play the game (and I use the word attempting very loosely) and when there was nothing more exciting left to do... and also collecting the ab&c football gum cards, a scattering of mid 70's Rotherham Utd matches and meeting their player Richard Finney at our junior school. It was a laugh, it got you mucky and if you were brave enough it gave you the chance to stick the boot into some big-headed clever arse tough twat that you hated and might not dare do so to otherwise! We would also take up our own version of Cricket that would almost always end up with the compulsory smashed neighbour's window. Can you imagine getting away with that nowadays? There was one particular close by neighbour that me and my mates must have put their window through at least six times one summer... and our parents never got sued once.

Other traditional school holiday pastimes were the local swimming baths sessions (complete with our eye-sucking goggles), trips to the cinema and apple orchard raiding (until one albino orchard owner took all the fun out of it by giving us a supermarket's worth of apple stock and spoilt our fun: though his all white appearance did spook us more than the farmers air rifle). The days of the classic kids matinee era were well gone by the time we were allowed on a bus to town, but there were still afternoon showings of most films back then and the six weeks holiday local cinema's schedule would be fairly accommodating with re-runs of Disney classics (Yuk!),Herbie rides again (almost acceptable) John Wayne blasting the Japs in 'The Sands of Iwo Jima' (Rat-a-tat-a-tat) and later on plastic Dinosaurs and magnified Lizards in 'The Land that Time Forgot' with Doug McClure (that's more like it): "Eh, that's that fella out of The Virginian int it?" shouted some kid whilst watching that. Then, on sighting the cavemen peering into the screen another comment came out..."Eh, look, its bloomin'

Freddie Starr." To get to these shows, we would sell, bribe and swap pop bottle tops at the shops to raise funds. On return from the best films, we would attempt to re-enact the best action bits and disappear into our own little world of adventurous action-packed fantasy, where only the pangs of deep hunger or the theme tune to Tarzan starring Ron Ely from a telly booming out of someone's house would entice us back into the real world!

A part of growing up is relating to stuff that goes on around you – and getting much of it mixed up and out of context. As a kid I only saw things through a pretty narrow tunnel, which was constantly expanding as I gathered more and more information about my surroundings and life in general. I laugh now at how daft some stuff I used to come out with must have sounded to my parents and brothers: but, then, I was living in my own little kids' world. I thought boys all had short hair; this being before kids – the ones I knew anyway – had been passed down any notions of post 1960's hippiedom and its associated long hair, though that would arrive pretty soon. At this point lasses all had long hair, without exception. When I saw a lass my age with short hair (a kind of post 1969, almost skinhead crop), I was mesmerised. Why did she not have long hair? It confused me a lot. Imagine the confusion of seeing our generation of lads suddenly starting to grow longer hair a few years on. Sometimes not much added up!

This blinkered vision was also set in stone for what I saw on the telly too: to the point of not getting undressed and into me pyjamas while the news reader was watching. His stare appeared to be aimed precisely at me, "He must be able to see me, he's looking at me." When John Wayne was in a cowboy film (we called all westerns cowboys, not westerns) he was called John Wayne. How could he be called the Ringo Kid as our Glen says he is called in 'Stagecoach'? Besides isn't Ringo that drummer bloke in some band that used to be always mentioned on the telly? Lo and behold, some fella out of Hawaii Five O' suddenly appeared in a cowboy film too. How could he have been alive that long? The cowboys were alive nearly a hundred years ago I had been told: they even rode around the old Roman banks just past the local park, so our Paul had said. But then, he had also been a commando in WW2 as well, and I couldn't quite figure that one out either. How come he hadn't been killed if he had been on so many dangerous secret missions against the Jerries and the Japs? And where is his old uniform? Christ ain't it a confusing time being a young 'un!

Speaking of war-time heroics, Jeff Chandler was always on the telly or so it seemed. He was a great tough action bloke actor to me and somehow, even though his full time job was scrapping with Indians in cowboy films, he also managed to be a Roman soldier who captures Jack Palance in 'Sign of the Pagan' (a film that always encouraged me to get out my Airfix Romans and set 'em up against the Ancient Britons, while our Glen was watching Match of the Day and telling me to shut up). In a fantastic little film, that I love to this day, called 'Away all Boats', good old Jeff also skippered a ship in the Pacific helping to land the US Marines on Jap-held islands. A good all-rounder, then!

Jeff Chandler (who died a young man at 42) had grey hair but he only looked quite young. Would I have grey hair when I am only still young, was a question that passed through my inquisitive mind once or twice. Anyway, he could handle mean old Jack Palance, so grey hair or not all would be ok, if so. Speaking of Jack Palance... the famous actor came round our end some years later while making a film in this country. Apparently he stopped over for a pint of local beer at the Rockingham Arms in Wentworth, only a relatively short distance away from me. How cool is that? Palance's foe in 'Shane' Alan Ladd was always on the telly too, 'The Red Beret' and 'The Black Knight' being two good 'uns, but I don't think he ever stopped over for a pint anywhere near us... not the real Alan Ladd anyway!

We had other proud moments of local history. Apart from our town's factory producing the cannons that Nelson used on the HMS Victory to bang out the French at Trafalgar and a certain Mr Bailey who designed the famous Bailey bridges of WW2, we had the Diana Dors-starring 50's kitchen sink 'Tread Softly Stranger' which included footage filmed near Parkgates' Aldwarke steel works and the old Parkgate train station that was closed in 1968. My mate John Harrison's dad was part of the throng of workers filmed coming down the road after their shift had ended. Apparently some other films throughout the years have included snaps of our town and its suburbs. 'I.D' the football violence-themed film showed scenes with our out-door market in and there are probably other claims to fame for us Rotherhamites, but we will leave that to the fact-finders and trainspotter types!

Whilst still at the infant's school, I had earlier made my first proper mates. First there was Gary Mitchell who had moved in just down the road quite recently. Our Mums hit it off – frequented the same bingo halls and probably smoked the same fags – so if they were friends, why not me and my fellow four year old Gary being good mates then?

Gary was as sticky-fingered with sweets as I was and through a mutual parent agreement, my Mum would watch me go to his house from the top of the path managing a play for a few hours: and Gary's Mum would do likewise. First pals sorted. I have sunny memories of us hiding in the grass of a nearby garden and recreating our version of Hawaiian music when young courting couples holding hands passed down the street. Why Hawaiian music? No idea? It was the closest we could conjure up that would take the mickey out of what looked like teenage romance. The concept of taking the mickey (or taking the piss) was not entirely alien to myself, but the outdoor version was something new. I quickly set upon a path of joining up with like-minded kids that were eager to laugh at, take the piss and ridicule anything or anyone that appeared to be open to asking for it, which was basically everyone! A fella would walk down the street with a massive handle-bar moustache and we thought he was hilarious; Pigeon face, the Peglets (a bunch of slightly older lasses who we tormented till the thrill of the chase) and many more. The name making and character assassinations would start with immature likeness's being applied to grown ups (i.e.: a bald man on the street was linked to Yul Brynner, but innocently became Old Brynner as we mistook Yul for Young). Sunday morning surveys – complete with pencil and paper – asking for passing people's favourite funny word(s) would eventually evolve into seriously immature but uniquely hilarious look-alikes searches. The game/concept/idea/occupation would eventually be christened as looking for war criminals; the relation of the title to its actual job description remaining a complete mystery, but it stuck.

Making names up for people has been something that has stuck with me ever since. It brightens things up, and I don't mind if anyone makes one up for me in return, though I would sharpen the laughs on theirs if I found out. It all started on those Sunday mornings when we were bored. There was Mouldy old Dough (after the Lt Pigeon record), the already mentioned Old Brynner was joined by Suckabogey on his bike who would get off it and chase us every time we shouted it at him, Reg Varney - Gary Mitchell's one that one was for a bloke who had a right pop at us for doing little Johnnies (sliding down the hill on the ice) past his house... he did look like old Reg Varney though. Also, the Omega Man, Smoky Bacon face, chewing nut face, Bonanza man, Blogged up chops, Alan Ladd (he had swept back blond hair so fit the bill) and later on Steve Austin aka Lee Majors for a fella that hardly looked like him, but somehow did fit our description of him as he had short silvery hair. Then there was the Doctor Who brothers, a trio of brothers who all looked like a different Doctor Who. They wore the same Dandy clothes along with the scarves and we almost believed they were from outer space. Their back garden gate/door was on a snicket and beyond it was invisible to us so it became compared to the Tardis!

Later on there came, what could be termed hybrids: a bus driver who looked the spitting image of both Victor Mature and Robert Mitchum became Victor Machichum; a craggy looking bloke we used to pass by was Leames Marburn... (A cross between Lee Marvin and James Coburn). The cast is endless and can be added to at any time, some becoming legends, some getting forgotten for a while or forever.

The thing is you had no choice, you got the nick name whether you liked it or not: if you were a fat lass with pure white hair... you were 'egg and milk', if you had blond hair and glasses you were the Milky Bar kid, if you were the lass with the funny eye who always played with marbles well you were now marble eye and if you were a red-faced bloke on the street with high blood pressure and a raging bad temper you were Geronimo. A kid up the top of the street had a really big head for the size of his body, there was nowt wrong with him other than that, so he became 'Little big 'ead,' No one was truly safe!

At this time we both became friends with Andy Goulty (a tall lad a few weeks younger than me and my new accomplice in making daft names up for people) via the infant's school and the convenience of him living right at the bottom of our street. Two became three and the fun truly began. One thing we had to get out of the way early on though, was the act of running away from home: me and Andy's idea and one that I would guess was purposely designed to do merely one thing? Antagonise our parents!

One day during the holidays me and Andy in a fit of parent-annoying enlightenment and maybe to stake out our newly-achieved six year's old independence decided to sod off. Not daring to venture that far, we hid in the garages only a few yards away behind the houses, laughing our heads off at our Mums' shouting us in and realising we had buggered off. My Mum's call of 'Toneeeee' earned her the nick-name from my mates as the opera singer. It was great fun and a real buzz and a buddy-building experience. When, after a couple of hours, we emerged to our angry Mothers, we got a short swift clip, a gob full and no stopping up to watch 'Appointment with fear'. Thank God! It scared the living daylights out of me anyway. I could hardly get past the opening intro of assorted werewolves, vampires and Frankenstein faces without being scared out of my short trousers. Nowadays I can watch just about owt... 'Hills Have Eyes', 'Saw', 'Hostel'... the lot – and relish any of the Horror films, but none of 'em manage to scare me like those twat's faces at the start of ITV's Friday night 'Appointment with Fear' seasons of Horror films.

Our poor old mate Gary! One scorching mid-school holiday afternoon me and Andy set him up proper. Now, back then not many families gave a monkeys how long the grass grew on the back gardens: as long as the front lawn was neat and mowered that was enough... leave the backs to replicate the jungles of New Guinea and war-inflicted Burma just like in the war fave of ours 'The Long and the Short and the Tall'... Dead alreet for us lads that. The block of back gardens on Warren Avenue was not nick-named anything from WW2 but was referred to by us as the Northwest Passage (after the Spencer Tracy starring Colonial days of America old adventure film) and if you patrolled 'em enough, you might well track down Rogers Rangers in that wilderness. There was a great little shop for refreshments at the end of the trail called Walsh's. Mrs Walsh was a lovely old lady who was very kind and wouldn't say boo to a cheeky spider. Their shop gave the name of the big hill at the bottom of Kent Avenue, the name of Walsh's hill. I would go regularly for a bag of Yorkshire Mixture and some fags for my Mum. At the back of the shop was a chiropodist, which was quite secretive. We would peer around the sweet counter to see what was going on, but to no avail. Could it be that this traditional sweet shop fronted a secret home for medical experiments on those stragglers who had veered off exhausted from weeks of fighting Mohawks on the trail of the Northwest Passage?

Anyway, our Glen had recently laid down some paving stones just under our back window and had ploughed some soil from the bottom of our garden leaving an abyss of a shell hole-looking drop down there. Me and Andy laid out some slippy banana skins amongst the blackberry bushes, prickles and nettles that loomed just in front of this big hole. Our trap prepared, we gave poor old Gary a shout from the top of the path and he came sprinting down like a madman - full of that crazy combustible energy you have at that age. Just past halfway down the main course and 'WOOOOOAHHHH!!!! Down Gary goes - slipping on the perfectly-placed Banana skins and gliding straight through the evil-looking nettles and Triffid-like prickles and wild bush and landing perfectly into the Bomb hole!! Tears of mischievous laughter and amazement at the preciseness of our trap and Gary's slide into the depths of the jungle hole were in full flow. It was hilarious, but we did feel sorry for him. Bit late for pity though.

Gary went home cursing: "Bloody, Bugger and pig" all being the chosen swear words of our gang - and we never saw him for the best part of week 4 in the school holidays. When he ventured back to our HQ after that, we asked him if he was ok and his reply, and these were his exact words, was "Aaah am alreet, just been picking thorns out er my arse nearly all week" His face was deadly serious: Gary was as dry as you could get for a kid his age. He never bore a grudge and even though we thought he would get us back for it, he never did. Great lad and a funny one too was Gary. He used to get in our tent on the front garden and punch, shout and go crackers inside it making it look like there was about six people in there all scrapping. People's faces walking by was bloody comical to see. When we used to get the soldiers out and he saw two that looked the same with the exact pose, he would say that they were brothers.

Another Six weeks holiday game we would play, along with the standard kids stuff like '45' and all that, was one exclusive to our little gang of gits. One of us would barricade himself into our outhouse and have to be laid siege to by the other two or three of us and try and keep us out. Of course we would have to wait while my Mother and Dad had buggered off to do this, but that was ok. Dad would be either at work down the pit or me Mother would be at the Bingo. Ok! Alls clear: Let battle commence. We would all take it in turns to be the invaders or the defender and, in hindsight; I still can't decide which was the best position to be in. First off the invading force would count down to 100, giving the defender some time to prepare his defence and re-enforce the door and windows from the inside. If you were inside, it was a mad sweaty rush to get the job done as best as you could, bags of old cement up against the door, try and nail some wood up against the small window pane and hope the sods outside wouldn't be daring enough to smash the glass.

The count was up and first thing to do was to charge at the out-house door and boot it as hard as you could a few times, in case the imprisoned enemy had not done their defence work as good as they should have done. It always helped to kick off the action doing that anyway as the kid inside would be alarmed at the sudden impact of the attack and it always gave you a buzz too. Cissy Bon Bon (The next door neighbour and a serious bingo rival of my Mums) would be most likely peering through the net curtains at the noise by then and thinking *"What are those Beesleys up to now?"* Next tactic! Go and get the coal shovel round the corner and give the door a great big bleedin' whack!! Right, that didn't work. Heads together time lads.

A few more batterings at the door to let 'em know we still meant business, and then assault no.2 put to plan. First though, keep quiet a bit as occasionally the besieged kid may pop out to see if we had pissed off and maybe make his escape. If you managed to do that (actually escape) you were the real hero and would get the annual Steve McQueen Great Escape award for doing so, which didn't hardly happen much. By now if you were inside, you would be getting just a bit worried what the next attempt to get in may be. You would be absolutely red hot n' all. Now don't get me wrong, we did have the occasional respect for each others property and we weren't in any stretch of the imagination vandals and hooligans... well possibly a little tiny stretch maybe... but if we meant to get in there and if the Council hadn't been out for a few weeks to fix owt, then the window on the outhouse would be the next to go. Smash!!! The shovels handle went straight through the window and pushed through the Cowboy fort base that had been pushed against it for extra protection. If the insider had any sense, then he would have seen this coming and realise he hadn't seen the green council van outside our house for weeks. He would get out of the way as the glass came smashing down and we would throw in stones, bricks and debris their way. If he was even more intelligent he may open the door and make a run for it, but he probably knew a sentry would be posted waiting for this. Another run and kick at the door while the window was being smashed and the siege would be almost over. In we would go and rough up the captured prisoner a bit - nowt too heavy handed as we knew we would have to suffer the same when our turn came next.

The mission accomplished we would go and get some ice pops and recover and get ready for the next turn. You may be thinking *"Well how can you win if you are on the inside?"* The answer to that is you can't! Unless you are lucky enough to be able to plan an exact moment when the attackers are off guard and barge out and make a run for it... or maybe get disturbed by grown ups coming to see what all the noise is about... but back then adults allowed kids to make a racket and do their own thing so that was also unlikely.

One of the Out-house regiment: Andy (Special Forces -So face showing not allowed) you can just see me peering around the corner

Did anyone get hurt you may ask? Course they did. You would get bruised, booted, choke on dust or a brick dropped on your foot like I did from our Steve. Or you might pick up the piece of broken glass ten minutes later and see it slice straight through your hand like it did with me. The pain was nothing compared to the fear I felt when me Mother came down he path from shopping and saw blood pouring everywhere from my battle wound and scream *"Get a Doctor, it's the hospital for our Tony this time"* I didn't go to hospital as I ran off with my wound and only came back to get it bandaged when a promise of no Hospital was made. A total fib, I am sure, but luckily the cut was clean so was bandaged up and WW2 plastic helmet back on, it was back to the rear for a while and away from the dangerous front line. As I said of course we got bloody hurt. We were kids and having fun and that nearly always ends up with someone receiving an injury of sorts! One bit of advice, don't ever try booting a large sized ball bearing speeding down a hill. I did. Just off the bus at the bottom of the hill I saw it speeding down Walsh's hill. Thinking it was a rotten old stripped tennis ball I gave it

my best Kev Keegan. Result! Extreme pain, restrained held back tears and a swollen set of purple toes for a good while.

Me and our Dave (Captured): I worshipped that plastic helmet. That's our Michelle's pram just off picture

One Outhouse v Shed debate between me and Andy, that started with me saying our outhouse is best – as it won't blow down cos it was made of concrete – and him defensively arguing that his Dad's wooden shed was the best cos it was newer and had a proper lock on it, led to us scrapping on his front garden, fists flying and legs booting out at each other. The sod was always plenty of inches taller than me and would find a way of over-powering me and pinning me down after five full minutes of us belting the hell out of each other... then proceeding to bloody choke me... My mate, Andy became the Warren Avenue strangler when you slated his Dad's shed ... but the rest of the time he was my *bestest* mate and we thought the world of each other. Why let a few neck abrasions that looked like I had survived a hanging at Dodge City get between damned good mates! Sometime alongside these battles for shed and Outhouse domination occurred the Boxing ring and bottle of piss episode!

Me, Andy and Gary, and Mick (who lived on the Crescent on the middle of our street) got roped in with this older lad who was, lets say very manipulative. He was always giving us grief and we, to be fair, gave him some serious verbal back, so it was six of one and six of the other! Anyway, this evening – red hot as usual! – he had set a boxing ring up on his front garden, which immediately got our interest and attention, while on our way back from the Parade (local shops). This time he seemed a bit friendlier and invited us lot over for a bash around, promising nobody would get hurt or owt. "Nowt to hurt" we thought, let's see what he's up to! OK, what he wanted and what he got, for his own entertainment was a good scrap out of each of us: setting us up as sparring partners for a good bit of harmless boxing fun with a pair of proper boxing gloves for each contestant. We were particularly inspired by the gloves and the promise of the bottle of lime pop he had at the side of the ring for refreshments and built up a healthy sweat and state of knackeredness whacking each other round the lug holes. He was laughing at us and encouraging us, obviously getting a kick out of us belting each other, something he had wanted to do to us for ages. We didn't knock any teeth out or really go totally full swing at each other as there wasn't anything for us to get mad at each other for - for a change! We had our eyes on some pop for afters as the Alpine weren't due till Friday and all our bottles of pop (of all colours) was all supped up. We were desperate for a great big swig of thirst-quenching pop!

Now, don't ask me why, but something about all of this set up didn't seem right to me. This kid was usually the rottenest kid on the street with us and always had something up his sleeve. So when the scraps were all played out and we had all had enough and he offered us all a well earned swig of his pop, I declined. A good job too. Mick and Andy and maybe Gary all had a really good healthy swig from the bottle. The bottle of pop had some lime pop in it... about 5% I reckon. The rest was piss!! Half an hour later Andy's Mum was knocking at our door asking my Mum if I had partaken of this exclusive refreshment. Andy was sick as a dog and throwing up all over the place... I think either Mick or Gary (or both) were doing the same. The Mothers sussed out what had happened and if I remember right went and gave Fatso a belt around the lug hole too. Never trust a bottle of Limeade pop, it can have many unwanted additives.

We never relented on giving Fatso some stick for many years to come and received a few good hidings back; he jumped out of his bedroom window once to get at me cos of my piss-taking. I didn't think he would go through with it, but in no time at all he was holding me up by the lug-holes, which hurt like hell! Still we continued the torment and endless hounding of him and undeterred we never gave in... that was not our style.

This was a time when kids still hung out on the streets, and as mischievous as we all were, grown ups didn't bat an eye-lid at seeing us mucking around: Now we would get driven home in a police car, but back then, we were allowed to play out our childhood in our own kid's world. We had no intentions to do anything more than have some mischievous fun and take the mickey and we wouldn't have dreamed of hurting anyone proper or stealing anything more expensive than a pocket-full of Mojos from the little shop. In short, we were unruly, but we mostly knew right from wrong!

What naughty stuff did us kids used to 'innocently' get up to when we were kids and had no idea what sex was all about...? For some time I misled myself to believe that sex was something simply to do with pop music, that's how ill-informed we were back then, and all the better for it. Funnily enough, though, when we did get girlfriends all we did was say we went out with 'em and held hands and give 'em a rushed peck on the cheek if they were lucky. The rest of the time spent with them was taken up with telling 'em about what we knew about WW2 or Football and what next comic we were gonna buy. There were some exceptions to this naïve approach to good old fashioned courting. A few 'James Bond' types, who were good at everything from Football, Cricket, Maths, fighting and all round learning and looking good, also had a envious knack of effortlessly getting the birds. These lads may have been the same age as us, or thereabouts, but could have taught the Fonz a thing or two about courtship methods... bastards!!! I never succeeded once with the lasses with my invites of coming round to see my shelve full of Airfix models!! I also messed up big-time with a lovely lass called Jayne, who I fancied to bits. One day, she sent her mate over from the other side of the class to ask me if I would go out with Jayne and like a total pillock my embarrassed reply was "Tell her to go n' knickers." What!!! As I said the words I was literally booting myself under the table with regret... you live and learn. OK, that's the Sex bit of this book out of the way; let's get back to some good old boys antics again... sod the soppy stuff for when we are older!

Now, where were we? Six weeks school holidays! The end of that period seemed like the end of the world didn't it? For two to three weeks at the start it was like heaven, lots to do, the world our oyster! Get to the end of the fifth week and boredom has set in, the novelty has worn off and the holiday at the seaside is over and done with. The long summer walks, and calling in at the pub for pop and packets of Golden Wonder crisps and a sip of froth off a pint of beer were soon to be all done with. Kids are so bored they are throwing stones at yer as you pass 'em by: it's amazing how few kids didn't end up wearing pirate patches after the loss of an eye considering how many stones got thrown at other kids back then. It was common as muck! It seemed like a life away when we had broken up from school and we had played every game imaginable to a 1970's existing kid.

And if it was raining, even the morning episodes of the Beachcombers, Flashing Blade and Robinson Crusoe on the telly had become a big bore; the swimming baths are fed up with our games of red arrows (running from all corners and just missing each other as we dived into the shallow end and knocking little kids and Mums all over) and that feeling of a full six weeks of euphoric fun and excitement has subsided as another realisation sets in – schools not out for the summer no longer... school is back and NEXT WEEK too! The re-introduction to the perils and restraints of school life had one positive notion – that we were now in September and it would soon be time for the Finningley air show weekend.

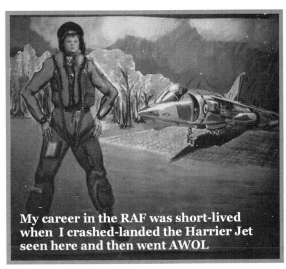

My career in the RAF was short-lived when I crashed-landed the Harrier Jet seen here and then went AWOL

From 1971, me and our Dave (and our Steve the following years: he was left in the toilet for the first one and missed it) went with our Paul and Glen to this superb display of aviation, stunts, mock battles and those Battle of Britain planes and Dambusters we had seen hammer the Jerry's on the Sunday afternoon telly.... Wow!

Finningley Airfield had been where our next door neighbour's brother had been killed when his bomber blew up on landing after a raid on Europe in the war. Its annual air show was something to look forward to and really get excited about and the thought of it took the sting out of going back to school. The first time we went the noise was unbearable and we almost cried with the pain of the amazing volume of noise from the planes in our ears. The next time we were

prepared and that extreme crackling in our ears was all a part of the experience. The sight of the famous Red Arrows dodging each other up in that blue sky, with streams of jet-stream invading the air, was something else. The Harriers taking off vertical was thrilling, the Vulcans zooming over-head and the Lancaster bomber landing with its rattling Rolls-Royce Merlin engines shaking the ground and the wheels screeching along the runway was a also real pleasure to see.

Me and our Dave doing our National Service in the RAF

Add to this the camouflaged soldiers charging out of the Hercules transporter and engaging in a shooting match (with blanks of course – I think!) was like seeing my toy soldiers come truly to life. And as you trawled around the airfield, you would see real life RAF men and women, just like in 'Reach for the Sky' and 'The Dambusters'. What a great experience it all was. A real treat of a day out and a great shame it had to end. RAF Finningley is now Robin Hood airport just outside of Doncaster.

Another great annual outing would be the Herringthorpe show or whatever it was called. It was a well attended affair with allsorts going on and (for us lot) a family day out. We would set off on the buses with all our packed-up nosh and spogs (sweets)... Mothers nagging us to calm down and my Mum drawing on her fags and extra strong mints. When we got there, we would find a pog on the grass to set up for the day, us kids sat around shooting passing kids with our pea shooters while no-one was looking. It would be bustling with people and excitement would be high... programmes would be handed out and we would scour through them for all the most exciting stuff that was going to happen.

The attending crowds of excitable people were typical 1970's. All the young blokes looked like they had walked off an episode of 'Man about the House'; the women with their plastic rain Macs and neck scarves and/or huge 70's beehives that defied gravity (I half expected a wriggling venomous snake to unwind out of some of the seriously constructed ones)... and old Granddads with their white shirts rolled up and ankies on their heads. Kids with basin-cut hair and 2 inch-thick crappy corduroy kecks: Bloody hell! Didn't we have the fashion world reeling, us in bleedin' Rotherham?

A great scène to watch was when the cops would re-enact a burglar scene and set their Alsatian dogs on a bloke running off with a Michelin outfit on. Christ them dogs were bloody good, but they must have wore some of their canines out on those tough fat arms of the dirty thief rolling over all over the grass trying to look like he was trying to get away. What exactly had he nicked anyway? I never saw him with owt? Maybe the poor bloke was some left-over drunk from the night before that they chucked in for punishment? Or maybe that was what the David Hemmings look-alike was waiting about for? Oh, he was a Hell's Angel! Anyway, it was fun!

The sounds of half of Rotherham shouting "Go n' get the bastard" to those Baskerville dogs would be second in excitement levels to the main thing that most people looked forward to at the show... the Motorcycle team lot! These fellas were related to the cops, I think, and were great on their bikes. They would set their bikes going and end up with around twelve of their mates stood on top of 'em. They could also ride through rings of fire, up a ramp and over parked cars and go at a faster speed than us kids at the mention of a pack of Spangles going for nowt! Speaking of sweets, I always thought that their helmets looked like Mint Imperials. They also looked just like the same bike riders on my Hurricane 1970 annual front cover too. They must have been busy fellas. This was a great day out and cost hardly anything: they weren't daft our parents, you know!

The famous Rotherham procession that paraded through the town centre to the endorsement of the Mayor and a crowd of excitable families also gave us something to watch, and again was a low-costing event to drag us kids along to see. Naturally, I was on the look-out for that elusive float with a full company of Royal Marines in full battle gear poised just like the front of an Airfix box of soldiers. If they had appeared I would have tried to climb up and join them, ready for some action... machine-gunning the enemy as we passed them idly supping Brook's coffee and catching them off their guard: my 'Billy Liar' fantasies could then be brought to life! Of course, every single year, or so it seemed at the time, it pissed itself down good and proper and we went home soaked from head to toe!

The Rotherham Centenary Procession 1971 passing through the town
centre in view of the Mayor
(Photo courtesy of Sheffield Newspapers)

Chapter Four

Junior School Comedy and Comics

"As Glam Rock swept throughout the teenage population and camped-up Pop stars strutted their stuff on the telly, me and my mates were in Junior School and having more fun and laughs than any adult could even possibly imagine."

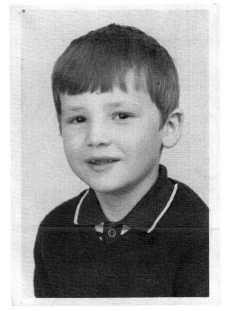

Short back and sides 1972

So, here I was, 1972, Infants School now over and the lasses' Wendy House went up in flames too (by some unknown junior arsonist.) Here was the start of my junior school years! What fun and mischievous mayhem could lie ahead of me? What teacher disturbing trouble could an unassuming young lad (a teachers words that - not mine) create within the next four years of my sentence! Well, we shall have to see.

Sadly the first year saw one poor lad called Paul develop Leukaemia. He was so clearly poorly and his hair was falling out and he was weak, but he didn't let it get him down. I tried to look after him best I could. Me and my mates used to play with him at breaks and make sure he was ok. We were sods at times, but we had good hearts too and we made sure he was ok. I will never forget the Monday morning I came back to school and was told that the poor lad had died. Up until then I had only known of my Granddad dying and I had accepted that cos he was old. It just didn't seem fair that this young lad had gone before he had even got through junior school. Throughout the years I have forgotten lots of old names and faces, but I always remember that lad.

I myself, felt a little insecure for the first few weeks at junior school. The infantile comfort of the infants' school and all of its relaxed learning and its sleepy mid-afternoon daze, although most of it proving useless for me, was now over and it was a further step up that rotten creaky ladder to adult-hood: though the very thought of being one of those big ones (that could grow beards and smoke and drink beer) was the very last thing on my mind as yet. So having to accept new teachers, classrooms, routines and God forbid NEW RULES!!! That made me feel just a bit more insecure... a dose of the Mumps followed around this time too, but I soon got over it all!

My first school report reads some signs of quiet rebellion going on in there. My next one reads signs of a restless, bored and slightly naughty kid wandering around the classroom trying to get the attention of the other kids... I was starting to get fed up of this lessons thing they kept pushing us into five days a week and, in my mind, had much better things to do. Morning Assemblies became something to inspire a restless urge to lark around, so pulling faces at kids who were in direct view of a teacher was amusing and passing little scribbled notes with insane names on them to serious and studious, well behaved kids, who would suddenly turn not at all serious on reading the crazy names, was great fun. The kids would get sent to the head teachers after Assembly pointing my way as I looked on pretending to be deeply immersed in the crap the teacher was spouting. There we were being fed all of this rubbish about how nice the world was and when we grew up all would be lovely and great, never once mentioning the Vietnam war still going on or why the IRA were bombing innocent people in pubs: course they wouldn't. They had to protect us didn't they!!!

And then, to make matters even more enjoyably comforting for us, they decide to invite the local budding David Bailey over to the school and line us all up for our rotten photographs taken. None of us wanted our photos taken and no amount of times of saying "Say cheese... Cheese please...." Is going to persuade us kids. "Just shut up poky faced git", we would be thinking! While Mr smiley photographer sets up his over-sized Crimean War photographic contraption, there's a queue of lads pulling the most stupidest faces we can conjure up. Those photos, when they eventually arrived in their sets of 'buy one for the cost of a home loan or buy the lot cheaper than owt' offers, caused more mayhem after school had finished than any other event. You were given them with no choice but to take them home and how the heck were you gonna get home without the rest of your mates seeing your excruciatingly embarrassing school portrait in your hands? No matter what excuse you had to rush home for, from zooming past everyone saying your grandma's on her death bed to teas' on the table, I can smell it... the kids were gonna see your school photos... and likewise, only the most professionally devious would escape the clutches of your grasping hands as they tried to hide their own away too.

And then there was Sports Day! The big school event of the year where serious sportsmanship and intense competitiveness came into being with kids faces suddenly becoming intensely serious for the fear of losing the sack race, egg n' spoon or shot-putt in front of their families and everyone else's families. My main concern was trying to take part without our Paul setting sights on me and putting me off with daft faces and general mickey-taking. One year as a result of my concern, I lobbed the shot-putt completely the wrong way and it landed full on onto the event host teacher's table! Apparently, nowadays, Sports day is a dying event as no-one is allowed to be a winner and there are no losers, in case of upsetting some kids and giving them a complex or something... jeez, the losers in my day, quite often myself included, would be ribbed endlessly and laughed at. So what, we obviously hadn't tried hard enough or simply couldn't be arsed.

Nowadays, health and safety has taken over the world and every breathable aspect of living is protected and covered or not permitted... just in case! Back then, us kids had telly ads that had the Green Cross code man showing us how to cross the road and the Grim Reaper scaring us not to go near dangerous water. Christ that advert sent the creeps up my spine.

It was a 1973 public information film called 'Dark and Lonely' and depicted the black hooded figure of the nasty Grim Reaper stood around ready to grab any adventurous kids who played in water. That fella was scarier than any future Freddie Krugers', Jasons', Michael Myers' and Leatherface protégés.... 'Clunk-Click, every terror-stricken trip!'

Back then, there were no real youth cults knocking about as such... not that we saw, at least. Obviously in nearby Sheffield and even some parts of Rotherham there were the Skinheads about: a keen bunch frequented the Effingham Arms in town so I was told. I saw one or two tough skinheads in Rawmarsh but I thought they were just lads who had nits. Glam Rock did prove quite popular and in 1971 on August 28th the ex Mod, part-time folkie turned Glamster Marc Bolan and his T-Rex gang turned up for a performance at Rotherham's Clifton Park. Looking back, even though I was too young, I truly wish I had gone as I did end up being quite a fan of his. Glam Rock was the name of the game for a good few years, that's for sure.

Then there were the Teds, but mostly they were oldies by now, yer mates Dads and older brothers and such... they were well past it by then anyway. Pop music and its associated fashion was all loose and party flavoured... but this was the 70's and teenagers and young adults just wanted to hang out and have fun... when the fun had ended, what would come next?

The next interesting stuff on the calendar for us school kids would be the sight of conkers on the ground, a new daft game invented or something similar... or if a new comic was due out. Well, while we are on the subject of comics, let's enlarge a little about them and how important they were for us in the seventies. I was seriously crackers on them that's for sure.

My first introduction to comics was checking out the colourful covers of my brother's Valiant and Victor comics that he used to get weekly and were stacked up in big piles in our hall. He would read them when he came in after school and then they would be resigned to make the coal fire with the next morning or whatever other household use was required. If I got there first, they would be safely kept under the settee or later on put with my own collection in the suitcase in the big cupboard. Our household must have received every issue of Victor and Valiant, along with a good number of Hornets', Hotspurs', Lions' and Tigers' throughout the 1960's. If we had kept them all, along with their free gifts, we would be sitting on a fortune now. There wouldn't be any room to move though, but so what! The thing is, back then, no-one held any value for hardly anything like comics or toys, models and their original boxes etc. We were, unknowingly, living through a golden period of exciting toys, comics and the like that were firing our imaginations, but were blissfully unaware that these items thrown around the house, crushed at the bottom of a toy box, left in the back garden overnight and played, read and battered around with use, would one day be worth lots of money and be high up on collectors lists. I lost count of the Airfix boxes I threw on our coal fire, the comics re-designed into twisted croissant shapes to help make the fire go on a morning and the Britain's Artillery cannons, Timpo wagons and Stagecoaches that got set alight by the hordes of Cheyenne Indians charging down our path. It's true; we set our toys alight with matches if required. That's what happened to my Airfix Bamboo house when the Japs laid siege to the Airfix 1/32 scale Aussie infantry trapped inside. It was set alight on the back garden. You wouldn't dare let a couple of kids play with matches nowadays would you, but we did no harm to anything or anyone except our prized wartime establishments.

My interest in all things war and action spread far and wide so comics were the closest, quickest and cheapest link to reading and discovering stuff. My first regular comic order was for the Victor, around 1970. Victor comic was the longest running and the most popular war comic and was published by DC Thompson, who also did the Beano, Dandy, Wizard, Hotspur and later on Warlord, amongst others. The comic, like most of its day, was accompanied by a yearly annual and a summer special. It was mostly made up of war stories in picture strip form and almost always the Germans and Japs lost the scrap!

Victor comic was launched on January 25th 1961 and ran for 1657 issues (right up until a last stand demise in 1992 - the annual bailing out with the 1994 one, marking the end of an era for boys' annuals and comics). A healthy mix of war (I flew with Braddock, The Forgotten Fourteenth and the famous front and back cover true life war stories), adventure (Tarzan protégé Morgyn the Mighty - my Dad's favourite as was Tigers' Johnny Cougar, another comic wrestling star) sport (Gorgeous Gus), cartoon picture strips with slapstick (Figaro the over-sized bungling Mexican bandit, Cap'n Hand, Ruffies and the Tuffies) and boys fave athlete... the eternal Alf Tupper, who loved Fish n' chips, long-working hours and a fair-run race. War comedy for any budding future con men, cowards and tricksters out there was provided by Captain Cadman, who took all the glory and fame for his WWI exploits, in actual fact dodging any signs of danger and real life heroics while his ever-suffering Corporal lived out the real action. There was the Hammer man who belted his foes around with an over-sized hammer that he worshipped and later on there was Joe Bones the Human Fly who could climb anywhere without fear- all for the Allied war cause. My favourites were Captain Cadman and Alf Tupper, but I loved any of the war stories that were regularly on the go.

Victor and Warlord comics: kind permission of DC Thomson and co. ltd

There's that old saying 'They don't make 'em like that anymore' which is surely true of the Victor. They really could not ever produce a comic like that again. Do-gooders would be up in arms about the eternally bad enemy depiction (the British were right, the Germans and Japs were the baddies and were obviously wrong); the bombing of Dresden would have surely been out of bounds for picture strip form too and the EU would demand a more revisionist and balanced approach to all sides being portrayed as equally good and bad. It would have drove us kids mad, that.

Like Valiant and Lion (No one could beat Captain Hurricane and Robot Archie!), Tiger (Skid Solo - the fastest racing car driver we knew), Hornet, Hotspur, Wizard (and later on Warlord and Battle) Victor captured a whole generation of kid's imaginations, in vivid artistic front cover colour and detailed characteristic picture strip form. So much better and far more rewarding than the toxic trance-like life-take over contemporary games consoles and mind-numbing virtual reality of today.

For a time Victor comic was the staple diet of all war comic reading and had the most sustenance, but the very first all war comic (with no comedy or cartoon diversions etc) was Warlord which was launched to a war hungry nation of school kids on Thursday September 28th 1974. I can remember being really excited about the launch of it and couldn't wait to get it.

If I remember rightly, it was even advertised on the TV. Can you imagine that nowadays? The main stories were Union Jack Jackson (The British Marine who, after his ship is sunk, joins up with the US Marines), Peter Flint (The Roger Moore-looking James bond comparative special agent out to thwart the Nazis) in 'Codename Warlord' and plenty of action-packed war stories such as Killer Kane and Tommy Atkin's War. Also on board were old Wizard fave regurgitated for 1970's consumption The Young Wolf (of Kabul). The first issue had a free gift and this was a gatefold display card to stick all the medal replicas given away with that issue and the next few weeks had a Super Swooper Hi-Fly glider and a Secret Sign ring and 20 stick on symbols. For us 1970's war-obsessed kids this was comic heaven.

The year after, on March 8th 1975 IPC magazines retaliated with their launch of Battle Picture Weekly comic. The war-themed treats were Terror Behind the Bamboo Curtain, The Bootneck Boy (the under-aged Royal Marine Danny Budd), D-Day Dawson (The soldier with a bullet lodged near his heart who shot his way through the rest of the war not caring less about the risks, treating each day as his last), the 'Dirty Dozen' inspired Rat Pack and later on such characters as Darkie's Mob and Major Easy.

which was a sort of Dirty Harry-themed character transformed to fighting the Germans in WW2. Everything about these two comics was exciting and made school all the more bearable as I would run home on my dinner hour to read on the day of publication. Along with the ever-dependable Victor, Warlord and Battle were the ultimate classics in war and action picture strip comics. For me they were the golden age of comics, no questions!

Battle comic No.1: Kind permission + © Egmont UK Ltd

Other comics followed – Warlords' companion comic Bullet (with it's Jason King look-alike star) appeared and Marvel brought Sgt Fury to a UK readership – but when a comic started to lose its readers and had had its

day, it was accompanied with the sudden special front-line news that it would be merged with another comic from the same publisher... thus Lion merged with Valiant then itself joined Battle, Wizard got swallowed up by Victor and so on; usually its central themes and stories, certainly its identity, being lost and forgotten about within mere weeks, with the exceptions of classic features such as Battle's Charley's War. In contrast to nowadays when every single issue of every kid's comic has a bulging free gift attached, the prospect of a clip together cheap plastic plane, Frisbee or badge free with our favourite comics was something special. Usually advertised two weeks ahead, we would count the days down for the freebies. When the short-lived Vulcan comic appeared with a free spud gun stuck on the front of it, every kid in the country must have bought it and engaged in a re-enaction of their most remembered historical battle. At our junior school the playground was full of lads shooting each other with these small 'last for a day only' firearms. The teachers never batted an eyelid and just let us get on with it. Think of that in this day and age? The weapon would be confiscated for a start, the kids dispersed and ringleaders recommended for a course for Psychological examination for wanting to replicate killing someone!

By the third term of my junior school years the rebellious nature of my inner self, along with a crazy and offbeat sense of humour that managed to spread like the mumps amongst the kids I could influence and get the attention of, began to take real shape. A little gang of us would open our school table lids and start banging them open and shut as loud as we could just as we would hear the teacher coming down the corridor. Before you knew it just about every kid in the class would be joining in and the teacher's face, when he or she walked in, would be a picture!

Teachers' reports of my defiance and disruption accompanied tell-tale messages of my refusing to do sewing – I mean c'mon sewing, could they really blame me. Besides, I had trouble tying my own shoe laces never mind piecing together a mini-patchwork quilt. Let's have a laugh instead. My anti-authoritarian instincts got worse and all respect for those in charge eventually disappeared completely out of the window with Frank Cannon! What does William Conrad's TV alter-ego have to do with owt, you may ask? Well when I was reprimanded for cheeking the teacher and sent into the corner of the classroom, whilst picking and pulling off classroom posters and art off the wall... I gave a sudden loud outburst of "Look, there's Frank Cannon flying through the window" thoroughly disrupting the whole gathering of kids listening to a reading of 'Charlotte's Web.' A future big mate of mine during the Punk years, Pete Roddis, tuned into the humour of that one and would always be grinning like mad every time I blurted it out after that. Cannon was one of a seemingly endless stream of trendy cop shows that took over Westerns during the 1970's and Frank Cannon was amongst good goggle box friends with a lollypop-sucking bald fella out of a Beau Geste remake called Kojak (had the board game one year, but only played it once before dragging along to a swapping session). Also, James Garner in the Rockford Files (never could get what he was up to, but the theme tune was good), Banacek, McCloud and, amongst others, Hawaii Five O' (with its symbol of Friday night's the weekend is here elation theme tune). Most cop shows were a big bore to me and didn't match up to a good war film, Western or belly-rattling comedy show, so chuck Frank

Cannon out of the window along with that mardy-bum teacher who is staring right at me!

Now, one of the favourite comedies of our generation of 70's kids was the Goodies! Right from the very first episode that I saw with the Jack and the Beanstalk story, through to the massive over-grown cat and the Bun fight at the OK Tea-rooms... it was all belly laughs and daft re-enactments the next day at school after watching the delights of little Bill Oddie, wimpy Tim Brooke Taylor and the mad professor that was Graham Garden. The series went along with favourites of mine such as the cutting sarcasm of Dave Allen, the crass but titillating (in all ways) Benny Hill show, the crazy unpredictability of Freddie Starr, Morecambe and Wise's clean cut antics and Monty Python's Flying Circus as the main chucklers for me. I came across Monty Python's Flying Circus one night when our Glen told me to check it out. I was immediately drawn to its whacky and insane off the wall brand of humour: some stuff did go a bit over my head, but some particular sketches I found hilarious... especially the M.J.K Pratt jungle cricket one, where cricketers were impaled with spears and the commentator's insane-looking head was lobbed off with a scythe. How could I not laugh at that? Monty Python was satirical and unpredictable and was maybe aimed at a student type audience of left field comedy thinkers. I never realised any of this at the time, but got plenty of laughs out of it.

There was plenty to laugh at in the seventies for a kid growing up, not all of it on the box!! The comedy shows would influence our following school day too. Back to the Goodies. One particular episode had the most far-reaching effect on both myself and the gang at school... the Rolf Harris piss-take one. This episode, from series 5 (episode 6) was called 'Scatty Safari' and first broadcast on Monday 17th March 1975 at 9pm, just in time to catch my attention! It was daft and hilarious and the sight of a Safari range rover chasing down Rolf Harris look-alikes (I think with a net?) had me rolling around uncontrollably all over our fluffy jungle of a fire-side rug. Our Glen was laughing at me and I was feeling like my last breath was gonna come; it was that funny. It was a classic and if I ever got fed up with me sen, I would always think of that crazy episode.

The next day at school, all the kids were talking about it and it gave school days a good boost for a while. Soon, the idea of laughing at it was not enough; something more had to be done to pay homage to this special comedy classic. I know, we can set up our own football team called the Rolfs. There was me, Gary Mitchell, Nicky Booth, Andy Goulty, Bryan Haller, Ian Cooper... I think our Dave and Steve and a few others I can't remember the names of. We set some games up and before you know it the Rolfs had a name for themselves in school playground football... we nearly always lost!! So what, it's only a game: how were we to stand a hope in hells chance against the budding Peles' and Kevin Keegans we were up against... we were daft lads, they were serious. But, we had some good games and laughs and never took it all serious one bit. It was all about having fun.

This fun was far more genuine than the pressure I was put under by the schools resident Kes-styled teacher copyist who used to bang my head between two studded football boots for choosing to spend my weekend pocket money on soldiers, gum cards and comics rather than a proper football kit. I hated that teacher at the time. He never missed a chance to have a dig at me and try and make me feel small... but I didn't relent. Anyway a letter from our Paul stating in no uncertain terms that he was gonna come down and belt him if he cracked me once more sorted him out. I wasn't gonna be part of his stinking team anyway that's for sure... and he had a chuffin' King John style beard too, the Magna Carta cheating sod!

Which brings me back to our bearded heroes the Rolf Harris's of this world. Not content with laughing at the Goodies, alone, or setting up a team in respect of the bearded artist, we now quickly set about laughing at every dark-haired middle-aged man with a black beard that we could set our sights upon. Bloody hell, if the cops had employed us to catch and identify the Yorkshire Ripper we would have pointed him out in no time. This vindictiveness towards the dark haired unshaven species knew no bounds. The bloke who lived at the side of the school passed by with a beard and we rolled all over the grass laughing at him and his beard... he didn't have a clue either, just looked at us all puzzled. The parents with beards who came around the corner before the start of the school day while we were lingering around taking the mickey got pointed at and laughed at very loudly. Then there was the teacher from the big school (secondary or whatever you wanna call it... it was the big school to us)... well guess what... he too had a proper Rolf beard. In-fact he was a dead ringer for the man himself. Every single end of school day, we would wait around to see if he would arrive to pick up his teacher wife in his white car. We would be waiting around the corner and when he appeared we would all shout "Rolf Harris, YES, its Rolf Harris!!! Look at him its Rolf." He would shake his fists at us and sometimes try and chase us, but he never caught us. He kept his beard though. The Rolf phenomenon never really died; it just got swallowed up with various off-springs and even crazier names and school playground cults... Rolf Harris even merged with Harry Corbett when we came across a bald-headed-bearded man... he became Harry Harris Harrison!

Our Dave, Michelle and Steve

One other laughter-inducing cult icon for us back then was Scooby Doo. No not the TV cartoon one (good as that was)... my brother's own Dog, Mickey. Our Paul bought a little Jack Russell puppy. It was cute as anything, soft as a brush and loved us kids and.... it wouldn't stop growing!! Before we knew it, the small cuddly baby Jack Russell turned into the Incredible Hulk of small dogs and was as big as an over-grown Labrador and beyond. It may have cost more to feed and took up far more space on the settee than we all thought it would, but it was worth its weight in Chum for all the hilarious encounters and funny stories that the dog created. Our Paul's dog – nicknamed Scooby Doo – became a part of our family's folklore and more than worthy of a story or two, or three. Mickey, or Scooby – he could do a genuine impression of the cartoon dog no word of a lie – well he lived at our Paul's with him, Megan and our Dave, Steve and Michelle. But I also spent a lot of my time there and it being a case of us kids being like brothers and sisters, me being the eldest. So the dog was partly mine too. It was our family mascot and I have never known a dog like it since!

Scooby led a dog's life of adventure. He lived an outdoor life when dogs didn't have to wear leads and the dog catcher was not fast enough to catch him in his 3 wheeler Reliant Robin. He was let out to fend for his sen and came home for tea time. He was the fastest dog in the West... West of West Avenue that is! He was always scrapping with other dogs, old Scooby, but he was no bully... no he would leave any other dog alone as long as they didn't stroll past him while he was on sentry duty at our Paul's front gate. If the dogs made that mistake then they paid for it in full.

One day, one of our Paul's drinking buddies, over at the Monkwood boozer, challenged our Paul upon his dog's reputation. "That may be, Paul" he bragged "he may be tough and up for scrapping with yer average dog, but he won't beat my pit-bull." Big mistake... showdown with Mickey the Kid v the Black Bart pit-bull outlaw at kicking out time was set up.

I saw our Paul come round the corner from the pub. Nowt new on a Sunday dinner time. This time he had a mission and a challenge on his hands: can his mate's dog manage to get past Fort Scooby? Black Bart the pit-bull appears on the lead with his crooked Sheriff and grinning clearly walks past the look-out post of Fort Scooby. Ears are up, nose is pushed out pouting and off Scooby goes. The enemy is dragged from his master's grasp and lead and dog are out of control and hand. The scrap has begun!

Without going into too much gory sadistic detail and not wanting to upset 21st century dog lovers with this tale of a politically incorrect episode (remember this was the mid 70's and we lived different lives to our Orwellian-styled modern age of now), suffice to say the battle was fierce and more than a little unprecedented by all. What was expected to be a tug, snap and a bite soon turned into what, to us, seemed like the fiercest dog battle known to mankind. Cricket bats were snapped and buckets of water thrown in trying to part the two opponents, but all to no avail. Screams and tears from the fairer sex were balanced by the sense of pride we felt for our canine protector who had shown his worth... "good old Scooby" us kids rejoiced! The legend of Scooby was further enforced into our minds now. Scooby was a proper part of our little gang and every kid knew of him.

"Whatcha looking' at Mister?"   The legendary Scooby

Other adventures of the battling over-grown Jack Russell that was Mickey were- getting run down by a double Decker bus full on and getting straight up and strolling off as though nothing had even happened; being looked after by my Mother while we went away for the week and almost killing off the local dog population around our street; a fight with the Black Devil cat that attacked humans up the street and a riotous havoc-causing visit to see us kids at school down the road. He saw us playing at dinner-time, one summer and launched himself straight over the school wall and knocked all the lasses flying to get to us. Kids were screaming and crying as he created mayhem- chasing us and everyone else all over the school field... he only wanted to play, but he did get a bit rough old Mickey. He didn't realise his own strength. Before long, the bell went and it was indoors time for us... Mickey followed. I can hear those teachers' shouts to this day as Mickey charged and knocked down teacher, table and kid alike in his over-active excitable chase frenzy. He was ragging kids' jumpers, diving up and knocking school books out of kids' hands; sprinting like crazy down the school corridor, skidding around corners looking all over for us. "Who's the heck is that damned dog" were the cries from the teachers: I could almost hear the theme tune to Roobarb playing. It was bedlam and that's the sort of stuff I liked best about school... when it all went to bits and the rules were thrown out of the window causing upheaval... to see teacher's faces getting all frustrated and angry and not knowing what to do was great fun... and it was our Paul's out of control rebel of a dog that caused it all!!!

When old Mickey died some years later in the early 1980's he had lived a great life of canine adventure... an enviable life of freedom with no strings or leads attached. The record 'Old Shep' by Elvis brought the house down in tears when it got played for him in remembrance.

Around this time, my Mum and Dad decided on having a bit of a house revamp. I don't know where the money came from, maybe a bit of back pay from my Dad's pit or a tidy win on the ponies, I dunno? Anyway, we were now ready to move into the 1970's with style! We had new carpets (the front room one typically soon got its newness spoilt by a lump of red hot coal flying out of the fire and scorching a hole in it, which then got sneakily covered by the toasting fork and brush stand), we had the typical 1970's style wood panelling fitted on the main wall, a new hearth and fireplace replacing our old 1950's one with it's inbuilt oven that looked like something from the Great War. We had a gas fire fitted in the other room, replacing the other coal fire and some trendy ceiling tiles in our living room. These were extremely flammable and a whole bunch of them, after being glued in place, constantly hung down in a threatening manner, their sights set on falling and drifting over to the rampant coal fire only mere inches away. When they did fall down they would usually land on my Dad's head while he was watching the Horse racing or reading the paper or something. Time and again they had to be fixed back in place: the price for upgrading! The room also became over-run with brass! Brass swords and guns mounted on wood panelling, brass monkeys, little brass curio ornaments... brass photo frames, brass ash trays... brass everything.... Even the shield of Ivanhoe on the wall, complete with yes... brass swords. The brass was everywhere. It needed cleaning with Brasso every now and again, it was always falling off the mantle piece or wall and made our living room look like an Antique shop but we were coming up in the world and the accumulation of brass was proof of that. It was like some kind of working class euphemism of saying "Look we've made it we're all brassed up!" Where once we were brassed off now we are brassed up... It was 1973 and we had arrived in the modern age!

By the middle of my junior school years, there was an inner core of loonies ... daft and crazy kids that would do owt for a laugh. I have to own up; I was one of them and usually in the middle of anything daft going on.

One of the most bizarre and (for the victim - embarrassing) new ritualistic games must surely have been the 'pulling the trousers/shorts down' one.
I have no idea how it started or who started it. The trouser or shorts pulling high-spirited ventures were administered at random, any place and in front of anyone... there was no mercy! The only rule was that it was males only; not for some injected Freudian male, dare I say, inner gay tendencies ... no not at all... it was restricted to the lads cos it was meant to show up the lads... in front of the girls preferably. Also, I suppose, we really didn't know what we were gonna find if we started handing it out to the lasses. I think everyone of us got trousered at some point. It was impossible not to. Lads walking down the corridor in line: zoom down the kecks went - leaving teary-eyed kid the figure of ridicule when the rest of the class turned round. Lads waiting to have their needle injections... zoom, down came the kecks. The only way you could guarantee safety was if you had fainted through fear of the incredible expanding booster... and some kid always did. Lad climbing up a tree trying desperately to impress the girls on the grass making daisy chains... zoom... and shorts were down- dodgy Y-fronts for all to see. Lad jumped on by his mates in the classroom, while the teacher had buggered off for a fag for five minutes... trousers down, lasses running over peering at the sight... turn around and guess what... the head teacher is looking over and watching to see what we were all doing. Whoops!!! Less than five minutes later and Tony and a selection of the infamous trouser pullers are coming out of the head teacher's office with sore arses' cos of the belting from the leathery 18th century slipper Mr Dracula himself has to his ownership... always someone out to spoil your fun isn't there? We did deserve it, though. On the subject of bending over, while our Scooby was around, we used to throw a tanner on the floor and wait for a kid to bend over to pick it up and old Scooby would be straight on there - pneumatic drill speed - the randy old git! It was hilarious and worth losing a tanner.
One of the teachers me and my mates had at this time was, let's say a tad eccentric. He was an old fashioned sort, funny without knowing it, bad-tempered and unpredictable too. He loved my written projects on warfare through the ages and the like and could have a kind word when you behaved... so not a bad teacher all in all... But a bit of a nut case. When me and my mate Andy had another fall out and had a proper boxing match in

the classroom, while he went outside for a smoke on his pipe or something, he came back to the sight of us both with bleeding noses and belting each other in the chops and the telling off we got was not for scrapping in the first place, but for not shouting him back in to watch. You really couldn't make him up. I busted a kid's nose and he blamed the other kid for letting me do that to him! Imagine being taught like that nowadays?

One day, I decided that I had had enough of school and half way into one particular boring lesson with the boxing referee/eccentric old cantankerous old git, I just stood up and upped and went. The teacher and kids just looked at me, thinking I was most likely off to the bog or something, though I hadn't raised my hand to request permission to do so. Well I wasn't off to the bog; I was off home and home I went. I got detention for that misdemeanour and when the end of the next day's lesson came and the time was set for my detention because of it... Instead I went home again, via the Parade shops for some spogs first!! Just another case of my inner restlessness and knack for teacher indifference, I suppose!

By this time, me and my mate Andy were at our peak of our long friendship. Our laughs were never-ending and anything could happen. We were young daft kids and life was great. Our interests were mostly the same, we fell out now and again and give each other a clip, but it would be brief, one of us calling for the other the next day with a sullen face saying "Are tha playing out then." So much went on, it's hard to remember a lot of it, but we seemed to cram as much as we could into those years. Daft as owt we were and accidents do happen from time to time.

Going to school after my dinner hour one day, I saw Andy still not quite ready for school and kicking a ball about on his front. As I arrived for him he was whistling the theme tune to 'Match of the Day' and having a great kick about. Just as he saw me, theme tune still being recited, he showed off his great volley skills by launching the ball straight through his front window. His face was horrified whilst my belly was aching with uncontrollable laughter. Another time when we went down to his house the door was locked so he gave it a good punch and that smashed too. We quickly boarded it up with his Striker board game base... whoops!

Games of cricket were played out either on the street outside our house (Cars were still relatively quite far and few between in 1973) or on our side path. The times we put neighbour's windows through was uncountable as the sound of breaking glass became the soundtrack to our games of cricket! We kept the council busy refitting new ones that's for sure. One time, a council worker came to fix one of our windows or something and he fell straight off the ladders landing flat on his back on our path. It must have hurt quite badly. Now, you would think, his first concern would be for his own well being, but the first words he said to us was "Please, whatever you do, please, please do not tell your Paul."

"Don't tell your/our Paul." Those words would become common over the years. If owt ever went wrong or you had something embarrassing to hide, he would be the last person you needed to find out. He knew no boundaries for mimicry, and I, myself, can't throw stones that way one bit. You always knew something daft would happen around our Paul, though. One day when we were going round to the pub for pop n' crisps for us and a pint or three for him, he had some gob-stoppers and spat one out, kicked off the end of his winklepicker shoe and it hit a bloke smack bang on the forehead as he came around the corner! Our Steve got a belt and a telling off: "Don't do that again, what have I told yer" Paul said. In 1973, the country was on strike and me and our Paul went scrounging around acquiring coal, but we came back with a massive tin of paint instead. Just like when he took us for chestnuts, we ended up getting chased off by someone, usually with an over-zealous Nazi Alsatian dog for company! "C'mon Tony, let's make a bloody run for it" the orders would be shouted..."Oh no, not again."

The strikes of 73-74 were known as the Winter of Discontent. The country was going through economic and political turmoil and in December we had a series of intermittent power cuts, often without warning. I can remember the hours of darkness and only a candle to see where we were or what we were doing. Dad on the picket line, no telly, no games and no hot food for a good few hours, so the only thing to do was talk and scare ourselves with ghost stories. Old Nick (the ghost/burglar/scary man) must have been on his way to our house more times than owt, but thankfully never arrived. Just as he started to walk down our path, we were saved when the electric came back on. And what's the first thing that you see when you switch on the bloody telly? Chuffin' Count Dracula in 'Appointment with Fear' that's who... aaaahhh!

One of the biggest influences in films on the telly, apart from the war films and Westerns of course and the odd sci-fi film such as HG Well's 'Time Machine', which always had a kind of intoxicating draw to it, was 'Billy Liar' starring Tom Courtenay as the fibbing two-timing liar of the story. It was someone I related to as he lived in his own world, much like myself, and he admirably got out of scrapes at each and every turn. 'Billy Liar' (or Tom Courtenay) was my hero for a while, the two were indistinguishable. When Billy/Courtenay got shot in WW2 classic 'Operation Crossbow' by the Jerries it was a right shock and that was the end of Billy Liar! And of course, the reason he got shot in that film was for lying to the Germans: good on old Billy!

The other film to have an impact was 'Kes' and also starred another lad by the name of Billy, and that was as close to home we ever got with a film at the time, to my mind anyhow. Released in 1969 'Kes' was directed by Ken Loach and set in the mining town of nearby Barnsley. A lot of its scenes were filmed in St Helens' school and the film used real pupils, real Yorkshire dialect and accents. Telling the story of a young lad (Billy Casper) who befriends and trains a kestrel and also depicting his harsh life with no father, a bullying brother and little future, the film is bleak, humorous and earthy. The original novel by Barry Hines 'Kestrel for a Knave' is still studied in schools to this day.

The world of 'Kes' was so reminiscent of our world it was unbelievable. After all the usual telly of Americans, Southerners and posh people, it was totally refreshing to see this parallel world, so similar to ours and what we imagined was identical to our recent local history and schooling. Kes does more to bring back to life the days of growing up in late 1960's and 70's Northern England than any history lesson ever could... plus it had Ivy Tilsley's brother in it- local funny man, Duggy Brown!

The kids in 'Kes' were just like the kids we knew, the teachers a characterisation of what we had heard our older brothers talk about during tales of their school days (and not that unlike some of ours) and the Mothers and Dads were just like our Mothers and Dads. The beehive-adorned mate's Mums who formed that long-winding queue for the local jumble sale... hardcore hagglers knocking each other all over the school entrance as soon as the doors opened... desperate to get to the bargains. Mums who looked like a mix of the Les Dawson woman, Ken Dodd and the occasional scary wicked witch. Dads who would turn up for open day either looking like a demobbed soldier with a 1940's short, back and sides or a rapidly aging Teddy Boy with a beer belly or a dead ringer for Charlie George with his borrowed sideburns. It all depended on what age your parents were when they had you, but you could spot at least 3 cycles of the different ages of Dads stood waiting to hear what success or lack of success their kids had achieved at school. Big brothers too could be like 'our Jud' and when you ever managed to be allowed into the working men's club and there was a club turn on... they would almost certainly look like the band in 'Kes'. It was also the accents and the gritty sense of realism that was something we could relate to, the kids with out of date (at the time) Mod hair cuts, freckle-covered faces and the regular presence of the pits in our lives. 'Kes' had all of that kind of world within it and ours did too!
   A different kind of world that I also disappeared into was the hilarious slapstick world of Mr Laurel and Mr Hardy! From first watching their 20 minute short features such as 'The Music Box' on BBC2 on Saturday mornings, followed by the six weeks school holiday showings of 'Way out West', I was hooked on their timeless perfect comedy. Less timeless comedy that I felt was funny back in those prehistoric pre-PC thinking days, but maybe not so now, are the Benny Hill show and Mike Yarwood but I never got why anyone ever even got a chuckle out of Little and Large and Cannon and Ball: stick them up your wheeltappers and shunters!

By 1974, I was obsessed with the 'Six Million Dollar Man' and a new kind of hero emerged in Steve Austin- the Bionic Man. Saturday tea-time became a no play out period for exactly one hour while I watched, excitedly, the adventures of this re-built Action Man and his super-strength scraps with the bad guys and Big Foot. I never had the Steve Austin figure with the winking eye, though, and no amount of attempts to nick the one the mardy little sod down the street had, ever come off. The kid who stood at his gate with his Bionic geezer never trusted me and my mates one bit and I can't ever remember him coming out onto the street once. Maybe he's still there?

This was almost the mid 1970's. All around us, a post-sixties world of Glam Rock, Watergate, Decimalisation, the Common Market, nationwide strikes and the end of the Vietnam war had been unfolding while we lived a carefree life of games, comics, annoying teachers and buying our first pop music records to play on our square-boxed record players.

My real introduction to the world of pop music was watching the traditional Top of the Pops on a Thursday evening after reading through the Rotherham Record free newspaper to see if anyone was selling any Scalextric track in the back pages. The sights of Wizzard, Sweet, Slade and T-Rex - along with that enigmatic strange man with the orange hair, David Bowie, dressed in high-heeled shoes, glitter and make up was the norm for a few years around the early to mid 70's. My brother, Glen bought all of the records by these artists along with Mott the Hoople, 10CC, the theme from the Persuaders by John Barry (loved that one) and Mungo Jerry's 'Summertime' little ditty. After going to see Rotherham play every Saturday (and Tuesdays) and come back with a selection of the latest singles, he would then have to suffer the teases of Dad's taunts. So the Glam Rock records would be my brother's solace on a Saturday tea-time.

My favourites amongst the records out during the Glam Rock period were Bowie's 'Starman' and 'Life on Mars', the afore-mentioned John Barry one, 'Children of the Revolution', 'Metal Guru' and 'Telegram Sam' by T-Rex, The Sweet's 'Blockbuster' and most of the Slade

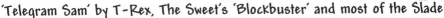

singles. Our Glen bought 'Old, New, Borrowed and Blue' (1974) LP by Slade and I would sneak plays on it, along with a selection of the other stuff I liked. We didn't have that many LP's in the house. They were quite expensive and a bit of a risk as often the long players would be no match for the singles. A Greatest Hits was usually a safer bet.

My best mate Andy Goulty would also buy a lot of records around this time from the Sound of Music in town and we would listen to his collection of Sparks, Mud, Suzi Quatro, Lieutenant Pigeon and that record about going to Barbados. He liked allsorts of pop stuff including Alvin Stardust, who also appeared in a kids advert on the telly as well as Top of the Pops. Another pop classic of the time that we loved was 'Billy Don't be a Hero' by Paper Lace, who we saw on Top of the Pops dressed in American Civil War Union infantry uniforms... must be a good band then, we concluded.

Carousel Tapes in Rotherham, a spin off of the Sound of Music record shop

This period was a strange time, but it was a great one. Style was all out of the window and anything went really. Joke novelty songs could just as easily make number one as the latest Slade record. Even our faves the Goodies got there with their 'Funky Gibbon.' Times were far more innocent, fashion was whacky, collars were huge, hair was long and wavy, Pan's People and then Legs and Co were a little embarrassing but beautiful and Noddy Holder's hat was nearly as high as Abraham Lincoln's stove-pipe one. The 70's were full of tack and laughable ideas and naïve innocent people and things but had better taste than the 80's and, in my humble opinion, much better to grow up in than the decades to come!

My contribution to keeping the world of music and the charts syndicate alive was via my brother's records, but my first vinyl purchase's were the

Best of James Bond themes and War film themes... both on MFP!! I would play these records, and my brothers singles when he was out, on my orange record player that would take about 12 records in a row and play em one after the other. I added to this lonesome collection with my move into trendier circles of music- the Top of the Pops compilations... Again on MFP, Hallmark or Pickwick? Not exactly cutting-edge hip Immediate or Stiff records labels were they, I suppose!

The famous 1970's epitomising Top of the Pops LP's were a compilation series that chose the most popular records in the charts at that time and had them re-recorded by a load of session musicians (the Top of the Poppers). Some of the interpretations of the hits were hilarious, a pitiful few were almost identical, some sounded like nothing on earth and an extremely rare minority managed to sound better than the original record and artist: rumour has it that some soon-to-be major pop stars kick-started their careers by contributing their undiscovered talents to these 40 minute ground-breaking suites of pop music heaven, one being a certain pre-fame Elton John. It is also possible that many more aspiring soon to be pop stars saw their careers take a swiftly downward spiral after chanting 'Mama weer all crazee now' for the Lord of Pickwick Manor!!

Conceived by record producer Alan Crawford, the very first Top of the Pops LP was released in mid 1968 with covers of hits of the day. The following year and a compilation was being released every six to eight weeks... borrowing the name from the BBC TV show.

The series continued, spawning many similar inspired compilations, and their front sleeves of scantily clad glamour models and cheesy song interpretations became as much a part of seventies pop culture as the work of the top acts of the day. The Top of the Pops albums symbolised perfectly the naughty tackiness of our 1970's naivety and innocence!

The rest of the poptastic mid 70's participation I indulged in, would be watching Mike Mansfield's 'Supersonic' and all the other after school pop music shows, reading Andy's pop music mags such as Supersonic's spin off mag and Disco 45 etc and being put off adult Rock for life by experiencing the Prog-Rock bearded (those Rolfs again!) long-winded meanderings of the Old Grey Whistle Test with whispering Bob Harris at the helm. It was our Glen's idea: he was moving towards more serious stuff now and had seen the eternal light with the most annoying long-playing record ever – Mike Oldfield's 'Tubular Bells'. My brother's hair was getting longer and longer, our Paul's was already long from the end of the sixties and I had noticed that by 'eck mine was now at collar length as well!! Static-inducing velvet jackets also became the uniform for liking the new serious Rock!

History teaches us that 1970's music and its future was forever changed by a sequence of un-related events and people seeing the light and casting aside the Adult Orientated Rock of the day and so on. Being a kid I never saw the New York Dolls on the Whistle Test, or Patti Smith's iconic performance a bit later. It would be another seventies icon – Marc Bolan – that would have a roundabout way of pushing me into my first truly serious musical excursion a few years later. From very first hearing 'Children of the Revolution', I was hooked: the whole buzz of that record, the opening guitar riff and Marc's voice is something else. I have our Glen to thank for introducing me to T-Rex and in a round about unintentional way, my quest to hear more songs that spoke of youthful revolution!

Before that, though, I had to plough my way through Smokie, Abba, Donna Summer and a whole empire of pop music, plastic Soul and throwaway disco to get to the real starting block. Even so, my rack of records was boosted when our next door neighbours' lad, Kev, gave me a few hundred 7 inch singles of allsorts of styles, ranging from Folk Rock, sleazy sounding songs, chart hits, Average White band, Creedence Clearwater Revival, some more Bowie and Bolan stuff along with Bill Withers, Cher's 'Gypsies, Tramps and Thieves', Billy Preston and much more stuff I had never heard before. It was all a musical learning curve; plus it made my collection look just that bit more worthwhile.

I suppose the music of my childhood was mostly harmless throwaway stuff, or at least the stuff we got to hear of anyway: the only real exceptions being the afore-mentioned Bowie, Bolan, Mott the Hoople and some of the classier Glam Rock stuff. More often than not it was a case of a soundtrack of Slade, Terry Jacks 'Seasons in the Sun', 'Crazy Horses' by the Osmonds and the sickly 'I'd like to Teach the World to Sing in Perfect Harmony' by the New Seekers (remember that Coca Cola ad?) which actually came in an all colour picture sleeve. I kept my records, lots of them not even in sleeves of any kind, in a typical tacky 70's record rack, singles on the top and a few LP's on the bottom. I thought I had the world with that record collection!

It wasn't just the music though: the 70's world of cinema offered lots of class amidst the flurry of Blaxploitation and every other exploitation styles of film-making. 'The Godfather', 'Serpico', 'Papillon' and 'Get Carter' being just a few examples. Even the TV series were of a far better quality than most of what the Mullet-clad 80's would later have to offer... The grit and balls of The Sweeney (who can forget those mid-week blasts of in yer face cop action, its theme tune and Regan's 'You're nicked' catch-phrase) and the original buddy comedy of Whatever Happened to the Likely Lads being a mere two examples of great TV.

James Bolam and Rodney Bewes as the two pals trying to better themselves present the greatest symbol of 1970's TV for me. Just a few seconds of hearing that Manfred Mann-composed theme tune peels away the years like nobody's business... shamefully nostalgic yes... lots of laughs dodgy waistcoats and sarcastic wit too: bring back Terry Collier I say!!

In 1975 Lord Lucan disappeared and the Vietnam War ended with the fall of Saigon. The fashion of the day – in this country – was by now, admittedly, a fashionable peak of ardent 70's tack: bell bottoms, yet more velvet, platform shoes and a sea of denim!! Beards were all over, beards with soup and crumbs in them... fuzzy side-burns and even more denim and velvet. Male adults were almost, to a man, long-haired... and they had adopted and settled upon a style and look that would take most of them well into the 1980's. Us kids were not entirely drawn into the latest 'gear', and would often laugh at some of those that were, but, without consciously deciding to be so, we were as much a visual part of the 1970's appearance as the grown ups.

Seaside fun in the 70's

By 1975, my hair was now over the ears and travelling downwards and out at each side, creating a commendable pair of headphones at the side of my head: the short back and sides of 1972, a result of being dragged to a proper men's barbers for what I was told would be 'merely a trim' were now a thing of the past as I began to look like a pathetic miniature straight-haired version of a poor kid's David Essex!

Chapter Five

A Red Chopper for Xmas!

"It was the best Christmas prezzie ever! An amazingly cool red Chopper bike... just like an American drag racer and ready to bomb about all over on: life couldn't get any better than this, surely... WOW!"

Christmas!!! A kid's paradise- a parent's headache and wallet stripper. The time for good will to all men (yeah likely), the annuals that took all Christmas day and beyond to read... not like those hardback pamphlets of today. Scalextric, Cowboy and Roman Epics on the telly, the Morecambe and Wise Christmas special, mince pies, crates of Newcastle Brown for the grown ups and lots of supertastic toys and games and maybe a red chopper bike for me?

I don't care what anyone says... Christmas isn't the same anymore! Call me an old spoilsport, a melancholic brooder, mardy git and a nostalgic

fool... I don't really care; it's just not the same anymore... not at all! For all
the super 'cater for all' shopping malls, extreme technology and cinema
entertainment in your living room, along with smoke-free pubs, fat free
chocolate and low salt crisps... I wouldn't swap the Christmas holiday
periods of recent times for those of my childhood... who would? They would
be a fool to even think of it. Don't get me wrong, I don't miss the freezing
halls and beds of Christmas yesteryear or the lack of a remote control for
the telly, but I do miss our old coal fire that truly meant business when you
wanted to get warm and the excitement of a film coming on the box that we
had waited three years or more to get to see as opposed to already having
it stored away upstairs on DVD a mere six months after its very own studio
release. Call it magic, call it rose-tinted nostalgia, so what... those days
were bloody better times to be a kid. And... no one lived in fear of having
their homes and presents burgled in the weeks running up to Christmas
either. Do you get my drift?

You knew it couldn't be long for Christmas when the school party
arrived. Time to get yer name on yer spoon and rummage out some decent
togs for the fun-packed delights of the Junior school Xmas party complete
with super state of the art School Disco. One thing I hated, though, was
going to get new clothes from Bunny's across from the church in town. All
that trying stuff on and embarrassing chit-chat from the Mrs Slocombe fan
club member and her mini-skirt-wearing assistant. Christ, let me get out
of here and get to the toy shop. The school Christmas party would see us
be required to do the twist to Chubby Checker yet again, us pulling faces at
each other wondering what the hell was going on. "Why are the teachers
summoning us to dance to this strange music with a weird dance?" The
teachers would pretend to be nice to us, which was always suspect, but then
it could have been the Christmas spirit(s). I suppose it was a laugh but
nothing on the scale of the real thing, Christmas day, but then again what
else is when you are a kid?

One prezzie that I received for a very early Christmas, along with my
first Castle - which I really loved and spent hours of Medieval fun with,
including hiding stuff in the dungeon - was wait for it... a smokers kit.
Housed in a Sherlock Holmes style designed box, here was a pipe, a
selection of cigars and a whole host of exotic cigarettes. I opened it up and

set about the delights of the cigars first, saving the more sedate pleasures of pipe smoking for after the Queen's speech (which we never took notice of anyway). The wrapping was vintage and I sometimes wished I had saved this present for prosperity... yeah, along with loads of others that would now command decent prices at toy and memorabilia fairs.

Don't you just hate those smug dealer twats at toy fairs and antique gatherings dealing in pristine condition fully-boxed, often unopened, certainly never played with and giving any snotty nosed kid the pleasure of an hours play with- toys and memorabilia: I have been to one of those affairs and was outraged and severely disappointed to see stalls of my old toys being sold as new for unaffordable and ridiculous prices... tormenting the big kid in me to consider parting with my money to help recapture my childhood. The bastards! Anyway where did my old toy box go to? What happened to our World Cup 1966 Subbuteo set our Glen got me into and set me off collecting teams of players for Sunday afternoon front room games? How did my Mother manage to sneak my Battle of Britain film Dinky toys die-cast Spitfire into the rotten bin without me knowing. Christ someone kept theirs in an original box and this sod has got it for sale for a percentage of my next weeks' wages. If I hadn't been such a greedy little bugger I would have kept my smokers set and be stood at the side of them with my own stall displaying what us kids got for Christmas back then.

Anyway I loved that high tar smoker's kit and devoured every little inch of chocolate it offered. I did end up smoking in later years, so according to the no-all rule-makers, along with those Laurel and Hardy and Superman candy cigs, I must surely lay the blame on the smoker's kit: like hell!!!

Christmas day was bloody hectic for us. It would start the day before with all the usual preparations; me Mother baking mince pies, disembowelling an over-grown steroid-injected turkey and me Dad out on the lash... the excitement was over-bearing and I could never relax on Christmas Eve, certainly not when I was told to get to bed or that clown in a white beard wouldn't arrive with owt for me. He was referred to as Father Christmas and I had already met the old bugger a few weeks before in the town centre where he gave me a crappy little bag with plastic Hong Kong-produced snap-together toys rattling about in... but in my mind, if a bloke was daft enough to go out all over the show, the world over, with only a sleigh and some reindeers for company while the rest of the adult world were having a whale of a time, well he must have been a daft old chuff: he even tried squeezing down our chimney which was about as wide as a slightly over-sized polo mint and would have given him a scorched backside on landing at the bottom with our traditional coal fire inferno! Anyway, clown or not, he was good enough for me if he brought me some good toys and chocolates. So off to bed I went, a twitchy little rookie soldier amongst a massive brigade of kids the country over, all hoping for what they had wished for, during weeks of excitable build up, in a few hours time. Now the first time, I realised that all of this set up was a farce was when I happened to have a nosy in the top cupboard in our little bedroom and smelled the aroma of selection boxes and new sealed games and the like... wow!!!

A few days later, when all of this had disappeared, I half believed in the myth again, after being told on my questioning, that it was all ready to be sent to Father Christmas to deliver: why do that though, when they are already here? Anyway in my heart, I still wanted to believe in it so went along with it all. That is until, late that night, on closing my eyes and reckoning to be asleep; I heard the sound of two voices coming upstairs and the rustle of bags and the like. Through a barely-opened, tiny slit of a view, my eye caught two shadows enter the bedroom whispering "Is he asleep"... stumbling around, with the effects of a few extra shandys, they dragged a pillow case into the room and some other boxes and laid 'em all out at the end of my bed. These two Santa's little helpers were me Dad and our Glen. Dad was in his black suit, white shirt and tie as always, hair slicked back and smelling of beer; our Glen in his purple velvet jacket and also stinking of beer. They never realised I saw them and I never let on. I wasn't gonna jeopardise the chance of these gifts coming my way as soon as daylight decided to wake us all up to Christmas day... I never went back to sleep anyway. Those hours of sleepless anticipation seemed to never end!

Yes!!! It's Christmas day! The quiet lull before the storm of Christmas Eve would now be interrupted with a kind of excitable madness that was never experienced throughout the rest of the year as an extravaganza of unwrapping presents, creating a mountain of discarded trimmings and gift tags etc... voices of exuberance and adult cries of "Calm down, don't get over-excited" bellowed around the house... knocks on the door, telly on, batteries being searched for and the first toy breakages as some big over-sized bloody foot trod on that Britain's civil war cannon on the dog shelf (floor)... "get the train set set up then, the cats waiting to have some fun." Another year would be Meccano and one of the very best ones the Scalextric. This was all worth kidding the grown ups on that we believed in Christmas and all its trimmings. Our Dave, Steve and Michelle would be down in no time with their Mum and Dad and the bedlam of Christmas was now fully in gear. The excitement was too much, what to do, eat and play with next?

The 1970's were the true age of toys and kids games. Never before had such a wide-ranging assortment of readily available toys and playthings been spearheaded so aggressively and carpet-bombed at a generation of kids. From September onwards parents the land over would dread the TV ads proclaiming in a super speed and enticingly excitable voice-over "Have fun with this brand new invention of a toy this Christmas" and pockets would be stretched to the very limit as Mums and Dads attempted to hold their off-spring up in the In-crowd's public eye of haves and have nots of the Toy Kingdom! Flimsy, easily-breakable concoctions of cheap plastic in loud over-sized boxes set the pace for which game was in for the kids this coming Christmas. Gadgets, experimental commercial ventures, TV character-flooded infiltrations of average, and otherwise boring, games and toys were scribbled onto the seemingly, never-ending Christmas wants lists of the spotty, chocolate spoilt long-haired, flared trouser adorned 1970's kids. You know you won't fool the children of the toy revolution... no way!

From the forever broken plastic of Buckaroo, Mouse Trap, Kerplunk, the Psychedelic Spirograph, Battling Tops, Crossfire, the frustrating Etch a Sketch and the amazing TV-Depicted roaring wheels on fire portrayal of Scalextric and TCR, the onslaught was endless. Kids wanted them all and parent's income and own expenditures meant nothing. Of course, you got what you got, but you could only live in hope. Amongst the Christmas games I can remember receiving were the superb Rocky prototype 'Raving Bonkers' in which a pair of Robotic tough Boxers belted the hell out of each other in a boxing ring right to the bitter end of literally knocking your opponents head off (well severely stretching its neck and jaw away from his torso). 'Haunted House' (regularly standing in for a game of soldiers in which it became Army Headquarters), 'Tank Command', 'Bermuda Triangle' and a superb shoot 'em up American Civil war game called simply 'Combat' complete with a plastic gun for each side to blast your opponent away from behind the hills of the plastic vacuumed battleground base: one of my faves that one. A couple of other good 'uns were 'Stock Car Smash up' which involved you setting up two cars and either drove 'em straight into each other or into the wall. The result would be just like a proper car crash with doors, bonnet, wheels and the lot flying all over the place. That's another toy that wouldn't pass the censors nowadays. Then there was the Cadbury's chocolate machine which scroungy relatives had to pay 2p for a tiny bar of chocolate to drop out of the bottom of your money-making chocolate-dispensing machine, all raised cash going to Tony's charity for the old Airfix and Timpo soldiers veterans home charity... put more simply and honestly, to buy more toys and Chocolate after Christmas. That and the 1973 TV-saturated 'Flight Deck'. 'Flight Deck' involved me and our Glen (always involved with owt to do with planes) setting it up from the top of our stairs to the bottom with the not-quite that authentic Aircraft carrier's flight deck awaiting the arrival of a dodgy looking plastic Harrier on string sliding down the stairs to land. Setting it all up, the prospect of seeing your very own Hawker Siddeley Harrier landing on your own in-door Aircraft Carrier flight deck (especially how it's depicted on the telly ad) seemed right exciting and great fun. In reality it was not. It was not half as much fun as sliding down the banister on yer arse and landing on our best arse-grazing Axminster carpet. You live and you learn don't you.

While we played with our new toys and skimmed through the Victor and Beano annuals, contemplating which stories to read first later on and our Michelle drove us all bonkers with her endless mini-toy record player renditions of 'Three Ships a Sailing' the blokes would be off to the boozer as the women prepared the dinner. On their ale-soaked return, all would tuck in and a right old mess would be the end result!

The Christmas Top of the Pops was essential; the Queen's speech was not. We kids would watch the big film and faithfully copy any battle scenes with our new toy soldiers, though I had a hard job of recreating Robert Shaw as 'Custer of the West' with the confederate general that my Mum had bought me as her version of the yellow-haired general. "He has a beard he must be Custer", she would still insist.

Fast forward past the grown ups late afternoon snooze, the smell of sprouts being recycled, the big Christmas late-afternoon movie - usually 'Around the World in 80 Days', 'The Great Escape', 'The Way West' or 'The Heroes of Telemark' and it was time for the Morecambe and Wise special, as much a part of our Christmas as crackers, mince pies and Newcastle Brown. The only Christmas special that I missed was when setting up my new cheap plastic projector and trying to watch a ten minute film (originally 90 mins or more) with no sound and being projected on a wall in the dark. On setting it all going, the sound of the reels going round and our anticipation of watching our very own film in our own house at our own decided time slot (nowt to do with the Christmas Radio Times or owt), the crackling of the picture adding to the cinema recreation experience... and then the film starts 'I Killed Geronimo' wow, I may be able to re-enact this one later on with the Timpo cavalry? "Hold on... this is not right... here comes a bloody Indian riding his horse backwards... bloomin' heck he must have been training in Buffalo Bill's travelling wild west show for a while" I thought... "oh here come the cavalry... some action... wow this is a proper Christmas this one... yeah!!!"

Yeah the cavalry really did arrive! They were bleedin' backwards too all charging like mad straight back into the fort with a horde of chuffin' Indians chasing 'em back in .... Blinkin' backwards too; horse backsides first and running the cavalry straight into their fort. It turns out our Paul had been sneaking a go on it while we were watching Billy Smart's Circus and set the reels back to front. He came in laughing his 'ead off, the swine. We were cursing him. He had ruined our first show: who's going to pay to come to our cinema when you were as likely to see The Longest Day crammed into a 15 minutes shortest war film ever with the British army leaping back into their landing crafts... or Popeye puking up cans of spinach at every turn! This debacle of a private screening was topped off with Scooby Doo entering the room and knocking the projector right off the table and the reels of film building up into a heap on the floor: 'I killed Geronimo???' 'I am gonna brain that rotten over-sized Jack Russell' more like and if I were big enough lay one on our Paul too! Christmas weren't half fun in those days. Especially with the excitement of that miracle of our 'Tomorrow's World' like cinematic achievement.... The projector and a feeble plastic knackered one at that. I wouldn't mind, but I think the film may have been on BBC2 a few weeks later!

Boxing Day (Forever the day entrenched in my memory as the one where my Grandma gave me a good telling off for wanting to box around the Christmas tree with our Dave) was still Christmas, but a bit of a come down. The rest of the holiday period was great, but the over-excitement of the proper day would often lead to our annual Christmas fall out. No one got really hurt, well not that bad, but names were the order of the day and there would be more rotten so and so's in our house than there really was room for. My Dad was a professional arguer so if he thought our Paul was cheating at cards, which he almost surely would have been, he would not let up. My Mum and Dad clashed like hell. The one thing they did best and most consistent was row and disagree! They were like cat and dog and in-between was the rest of the family trying their best to fall out with each other too.... Often succeeding, and for the most stupid reasons... but there you go, that's families for yer: besides I think, truly deep down, everyone kind of enjoyed all of the arguing part of Christmas... it was a great way of letting off steam and giving back presents that you didn't want! We were a proper united family... united we row and divided we call! All of this and we were not even getting a sniff of what New Years Eve would bring our way! But, it was our family and all in all they were good times and I wouldn't change a thing about 'em.

OK, there was such a thing as toys and chocolate the rest of the year round: Easter, Birthdays and Saturday pocket money spends the most obvious ones. And what plastic, lead gadgets were we spending our pennies on the rest of the year round? Toy soldiers mostly! You can stick yer View finders (I had a Planet of the Apes one, but after a few days of the novelty it was thrown to the back of the toy cupboard, never to be seen again along with the board games and their boring instructions that proved to BORED games!)... Lego was fab and Subbuteo was often a good game... but one pastime that our little gang all loved and took seriously, was our toy soldiers!

I must have started with a bag of Crescent or Lone Star ones as there were a fair amount of them knocking about in my toy box for many a year afterwards. These brands were boosted with a load of them being thrown into the box at the back of my three wheeled bike early in the decade by a lad called John at the end of the street. Next came the Britain's swoppets-cowboys, Indians, Romans and Knights etc and then the same company's Herald range. Alongside these were the much-loved Timpo range: I remember my Granddad Beesley giving me a three penny bit to go and get some new Timpos from Fergie's shop on the Parade shopping centre, who used to have them lined up on a glass display as you walked into the shop. I bought some Crusaders and Roman Centurions with it. My Granddad had died in 1971, but my love of toy soldiers remained and that bit of spending money he had earlier given me helped fill the ranks that little bit. Timpos were unique. You could devise allsorts of figures out of em... but where the hell did all their guns and swords all end up? Is there some graveyard of plastic swords and pistols out there?

A toy fort similar to the types our Timpo, Crescent, Lone Star and Britain's US Cavalry served their enlistments

By now, along with the new Britain's Detail range (these were fully formed figures with a steel base); I had a great little collection of warriors and toy fighters as well as my castle and fort. It all depended on how we felt and whose army you were gonna be taking on, as we also had a large collection of Airfix soldiers. The big soldiers were ideal for outdoors and Airfix 1/72 scale were ideal for indoors... a table top battle or a charge up the beaches of Iwo Jima (in reality a few settee pillows moulded to effect on the floor). So some of us preferred the 'big soldiers' and others stuck rigidly to the

Airfix gang... me? It all depended on who I was scrapping with. Some kids like my Star Trek-obsessed mate Stephen Lewis, who always loved a good game of soldiers, could be depended upon to play a fair game. Stragglers who you had invited round could get end up being cheating bleeders!

Now, there was a kind of unwritten rulebook to the art of playing soldiers. If you were asked to come along and have a game of soldiers, you were privileged... we wouldn't just go and ask any daft fool with a bag of pitiful made in China replicas. If you were in you were in and you had better follow the rules: those rules that us (the commanders) made up as we went along! In actual fact there were things you couldn't do. You couldn't just set up your men and then start knocking your enemy down in droves and declare a victory. There had to be some semblance to the many war films we had watched. At times, for significant campaigns, we even set up the record player to play War film themes for effects... this was serious stuff and was something we all wanted to win.

One Sunday morning campaign (with my Timpo US Cavalry trying to fight off Andy's Britain's Detail Indians) took place on our dust track of a side-path (Our Glen later laid some concrete down so he could ride up and down on his scooter more effectively). As the cavalry chased the injuns up Wild West creek – real life dust blowing all over creating a dust bowl around the battle – Stevie from next door emerged and joined up with his pals (they were all teenagers at the time) all ready for a journey up to the boozer for some under-age boozing. Well they spotted our battle going on and the big kids in them re-emerged and in no time at all, they were picking up little stones and aiming 'em straight at our soldiers knocking cavalrymen off their horses straight back to Timpoville and Indians back into their hunting grounds and tepees. Laughing their heads off and obviously well excited this small gang of teenage wannabe drinkers wishing to go and be recruited into the big world of boozing, were once again toy soldier-entranced kids.

Another memorable campaign involved me sending a whole regiment of my soldiers (My Britain's detail range now, Timpo lads being sent back to either the fort or West point for some re-training) all the way down our street chasing Andy's Indians and Comanchero outlaw friends. When Irish John walked by, he asked if we needed any reinforcements. We had already, cruelly told him that he wasn't welcome to play along with us and he could shove off with his Irish mabs (marbles) so the trail of the Warren Avenue trek of many broken soldiers wasn't going to be needing his help. Later on, I felt really rotten for that horrible and spiteful treatment of a kid, it was wrong and cruel but that's what you're like as kids. We laughed at allsorts, though: a bloke round the corner who set himself on fire falling asleep with his fag in his hand (he survived) and another fella who threw himself through the front window cos the ornaments were apparently laughing at him! Cruel but funny. Your conscience is still in development at that age, and than again some bleeders we knew never even grow one at all!

When we got to the bottom of the street, past nagging housewives and blokes on the way to the boozer, Andy had a whole new nation of Indians waiting for my expedition all carefully placed on the ramparts of his gate, giving us a welcoming ambush for our troubles. My soldiers were quickly knocked off one by one until only a handful were left to return to the fort up the street. Those Timpo guys had the right idea, stopping back for sentry and guard duty. Andy's Indians celebrated for hours around their totem poles and Andy, himself; well he was proud of that one!

Towards the end of those Indian wars of ours, we decided to re-enact General Custer's last stand on my back yard. He brought every single one of his Indians up and I loaned him all of mine. Emptying the toy box, we managed to gather about two hundred cavalrymen, including Confederates, Union and the odd miserable cowboy with nowt else to do. We set it all up looking fantastic. Even my Dad commented on its historical John Wayne-like accuracy. The battle commenced and in no time, the rules were being broken indiscriminately... by both of us. This battle meant a lot to both of us and we were frantically knocking each other's forces over with no regard for what would usually deem to be right and accurate... heaps of 'em were being first pushed over, then violently knocked over and finally booted over as we both stood up and joined in the battle in person and had another of our little scraps again. Neither General Custer or Sitting Bull won or lost the battle that day, though I could name two over-excitable kids who caught a bruise or three whilst over-looking the battle of the Little Big Horn!

During these wars, it became common practice for us to actually take things a bit too far and bury our dead soldiers after the battle. The family would look out of the window as me, my mates and our Dave and Steve could be seen digging real graves for our brave fallen heroes, saluting them as the Last Post was whistled out from our Sherbet-smothered gobs: years later quite a few of these guys would be re-interned when the garden was dug over and well into the 1990's and beyond the occasional soldier has been discovered in our Paul's back garden. It was all in the name of authenticity. Also, it wasn't enough to be recruiting rookie Airfix soldiers to my regiments. I had to set up my own tank, plane and battleship factory to provide the required military back up to support the lads in action.

Time erodes my memories of which were my first models actually bought and assembled (the word assembled to be used as loosely as the pilot supposedly fixed into the Mosquito cockpit me and our Glen built one time). Speaking of our Glen, he built a larger scale HMS Victory: well it could have been the Cutty Sark or a Spanish twat's boat for all I knew... but I remember it as the great immortal HMS Victory. I helped with glue application and confidence building as those tricky little tiny cannons had to be glued into place and the masts had to be held in position before the plastic sales were put into place. I think that was my first experience of a model set being constructed. I also learnt how to curse and lose my rag with half-assembled glue-smothered bits of plastic that day too, courtesy of my big bruv. In following times I built HMS Hood and the nasty Bismarck, HMS Warspite, the Ark Royal. Tanks such as the trusty Sherman the schizophrenic Lee/Grant tank, the lethal German Tiger tank, island hopping US Marines Landing Craft and I have still never built a Japanese Chi-Ha tank – maybe one day? The smell of glue was intoxicating and gave me a buzz. Little did we realise the dangers of sniffing the stuff back then. The Ramones had not written any odes to the pastime as yet either. When dear old Doctor Paise, the Indian Doctor who was almost becoming a member of the family from his ever more frequent visits to see my poorly Dad stopped in his tracks to watch over me fitting the final pieces to HMS Belfast one evening, he remarked to my Mum that I was a very clever young lad and would go on to University and great things... oh how wrong could a fully paid Doctor be with his prescription? Anyway, the regiments, the 8th army, Normandy landing forces and Commandos and the gang had their armour, navy and airforce to give them a helping hand in all future conflicts... the tank tracks being fixed together had been infuriating to fix and the pilots of the Royal Airforce (and certainly the enemy) would probably struggle to see through those glue-smeared cockpits, but the forces were ready for battle... All thanks to that great British institution Airfix!

One year, around 1975 (which was my last year for being bought toys for Christmas), the whole issue of toy soldier warfare and how to conduct it, was changed forever with the introduction of the Airfix Combat set. The Airfix Combat set comprised of a lay out battlefield made of card, a battle --scarred Farm house, two opposing sets of soldiers (British Para's and German infantry) and a tank apiece. To complement all of this there was some cardboard defence walls and plastic sandbag positions, but most of all, and quite groundbreaking at the time, was the introduction of the firing pillbox!!! Yes FIRING pillbox!!! Add this to the two surviving revolvers of the earlier 'Combat' game that shot plastic bullets out and you had the makings of a battleground reality. Exciting times ahead then?

We had seen those adverts in the back of the American DC Sgt Rock comics that showed depictions of battle sets which included exploding bridges and tanks, real explosions and the like, firing my imagination even further on how close I could take my wargames to the real thing. But, I never did quite believe those typically American braggart boasts of the real thing ready to be played out on your table top. Besides they also said they would sell you 'Real live sea monkeys' and 'sea horses that came alive in water' and also the products were out of reach anyway... we had no idea how to convert their dollars into English pounds and pennies. Anyhow in a timely act of compensation Airfix had unleashed a whole new set of rules. The pillbox in the new Combat attack set had something we had never had in our toy boxes before: it had a opening hatch where you put in your discs (ammo) and it fired, with the use of a lever at the back, these discs at the enemy soldiers– which means that the soldiers genuinely got shot and depended on the quick-fire skills of the shooter and not the military maps of correct procedure that we had followed all of these years... like the atomic bomb in 1945 and the nuclear age that followed it, our world of toy soldiers warfare was changed forever that Christmas day I got the Airfix Combat set. And it now meant that our poor little Steve had a fair chance of a fair battle against us, whilst eternally being forced to command the Germans!

When you're a kid, the lure of swapping stuff you may (or may not) play with is too much to resist. A box of Dinky cars for some new recruits to your toy soldier army is an exciting prospect on a droll Sunday afternoon. Or that Jag annual my mate Andy has, that I had my eyes on all of the year of 1972 with its amazing war depicting cover: well, he can have my Tiger 1972 annual for that one, a fair swap!

It had to be Sunday afternoons, for swapping. There was too much other stuff going on over the rest of the weekend, from Friday tea-times school release and Crackerjack at 5 o'clock to Saturday night at the movies and all sorts of games, scuffles and kids stuff in-between. Sundays were just right. So with the stink of Sunday dinners still vacuuming the air, we would meet up at one of our houses with a bag (or more) of stuff to swap. Those swapping sessions preceded Noel Edmond's Multi coloured swap shop by at least four years too. Keith Chegwin never paid us a visit though!

Me Mum and Dad used to laugh at me gathering my unwanted toys and stuff together to take and swap. They would say "Tony, you would swap us if you got half a chance." Mum won a portable telly from the Bingo in Parkgate (the one she never went in, ha!). She never went in the Sunspot Bingo in town either, but funnily enough everyone that ever went in there knew my Mum by her first name. The TV was quite a novelty. I didn't know anyone with a portable at the time, so loved the idea that I could have a row with everyone in the house and bugger off with my telly to watch 'Candid Camera' on me own on a Saturday tea time while the grown ups watched New Faces or something equally boring. With a bit of playing around with it I could tune into Anglia TV which broadcast different films, so on a Monday morning I could go to school and say "Did you see 'Taza son of Cochise" on Saturday afternoon on the telly' and nobody else had seen it... ha ha bloody ha! The portable telly fascination didn't last too long, though, as that went in a swapping session too: I think I got a whole fiver for it. In later years when I would complain as to where all my stuff went, my Mum's token answer would be "Well, you probably swapped it all, just like you did with that portable telly I won you." In fact some little kids down the street would be playing with me old Lego when I walked by or the bin man would drop half of HMS Hood as he was going up the path. Once, when I accused Mum of throwing out HMS Victory, which I swore she had done, she came back in the house ten minutes later with it in a bag, saying "Here it is, it was in the cupboard, you had packed it up to swap." "Yeah sure Mother, who was that roller-pinned shadow scuffling around outside near our bin, then."

My Dad loved the boozer and being with his mates and my mum loved bingo, fags and baking. Our next door neighbour, who I nick-named Cissy Bon Bon, as she was always offering us all sweets and salted nuts, also loved baking bread. Mum and Bon Bon were sometimes good friends but more often bitter rivals with a lot of aspects of working class housewifery, and baking bread was top of the list. Hence the bread cake wars!

It was almost always a Sunday afternoon pastime for them, though each of them could pull a flank attack and choose a different day of the week out of the blue, causing much strife and panic upon the aroma of bread being baked floating across from next door and vice-versa. After Sunday dinner had been polished off and the ice cream man had been and gone and Dad had buggered off to bed to sleep off the lunchtime session, then the dough moulding begun in earnest. I would come in from the street after smelling the bread being made and keep asking how long before the bread cakes would be ready. As soon as they were, that was it. I would be tucking into them straight out of the oven, red hot fresh home-made bread. Ten minutes later, with a stomach resembling a hot air balloon, I would just about make it back up the path to see how the game of footie or 45 was getting on, maybe I would have to sit out the next game. If someone had prodded me, I would have erupted like the Hindenburg disaster! Can you imagine my face, when Cissy would open the door and proudly proclaim her bread cakes were done and how many would I like to try?

Now, they both thought that they could make the best bread. Cissy would come round and bang a bag of hers on the table for me and our

Glen... "Here, my best bread cakes to eat, let me know if you want any more." She would remark. "You know I can make the best ones, Eileen will reach my standard one day." Umm, Mum's face would be a picture, no words would be required!

It wasn't just the bread, though. It was everything they did. The bread cakes just symbolise their long-standing rivalry. If we got a new carpet, she would be round for inspection before the delivery driver had even got back in the van. If we cut our garden, hers would be done within the hour and so on. It was harmless, mostly, and no real malice meant. Occasionally they would fall out proper, though, and a few choice words and even a flaying punch or two landed from our side of the fence to the other. The bread cake wars would involve spying, cheating, over-cooking, sad dough and sad bread, rock cakes masquerading as bread and the slamming of doors in disgust. In the end, though, no one really got hurt and my belly deflated eventually.

....

None of us were over-fond of school, but in all fairness the years at the junior school were, by and large, fun times and amongst the best times of our lives. The laughs we had at school made up for the long boring hours of lessons, the monotony, of which, was also broken by larking around and at my best or worst, I had the knack of disrupting the whole class. I can't explain why I just couldn't knuckle down and get my work done and simply behave. I just had this endless restlessness that would surface most when being presented with the more mundane end of schooling. As long as my mind was occupied, all was fine. It was when it had shut off from what we were being taught that I got this urge to mess around. Then again, my distractions could occasionally be the result of my own mind working overtime in its imagination department. I can remember one mind-numbing lesson and being in a daze as the rest of the class continued their lessons. I suddenly had a vision of the sunken eyed woman (remember, her from the market) and her pitch-black eye falling out and me being made to eat it! I suppose in todays keenly observed and even quicker analysed times, I would be certified as a Attention Deficiency syndrome badge holder or possessing of a disturbed mind? But, I can tell, you now... that was not the case, I was plain and simple bloody bored!

Bored or not with school lessons, as I say, those days were still full of endless days of fun. Out of school, every evening contained some source of excitement, or so it seemed at the time. Me and Andy had our dens over at the garages for our post-school base. We had been told not to go around to those garages, which encircled an old mine shaft, as they were dangerous. Our parents may as well have told us owt but that. The lure of danger and mystery to a kid is overwhelming. We just had to explore.

The lure of the old mine shaft warranted a curious investigation as did the council rented garages which were occupied with car owner's cars, a good few of them were up for grabs, though and were really easy to break in and check out. Made of corrugated sheets of thin steel, you could prize open the sides of them and slip in quick easily. Inside there was our own private little world and we planned out lots of our forthcoming ventures within those corrugated walls. Of course venturing up that way, although very close to our homes, could be perilous at times as the other gangs of kids, most of 'em older, also had designs on a garage or two. Sometimes they would hear us laughing inside the garages and try and scare us, but I had heard enough ghost-imitating noises from my brothers when I was in bed and they were trying to scare me, to take notice of their howls and supernatural copying. We were more scared of meeting them face to face to be honest. This could involve threats; a salvo of stones hurled our way as we made our escape across the gardens out of their range or something as downright spiteful as taking your bike to pieces, which did actually happen... the swines! But, mostly, as long as we didn't emerge out of the garage while those cut-throats were knocking about, we would be safe in our den, reading stolen commando comics which we acquired from another kid's den.

One day, in our rudimentary pretend-outlaw shelter, we realised that we needed some form of transport to make our getaways quicker from any raids that we made in any other territories. We had tried using my 3-wheeler (with its handy back compartment big enough to fill with any booty), but we were getting too old and big to ride it two mana! Our Glen was now a fairly experienced joiner and good at it too, so we figured to go and ask him if he would make us a bogey. He built us one alright and it looked the perfect image of showcase woodworking joinery. A large steering wheel made from an old bike wheel and some cool-looking wheels. We couldn't wait to kick-start our adventures on this new mean machine of ours.

Our first journey off on the Harley Davidson of bogies was given a push from the pits from the local bad boy of the street, who was always cool with us, despite a reputation to rival Billy the Kid. He gave us a great big smile, a great big push and off we went. We turned the corner at the top of our street and decided to take on the steep hill of Kent Avenue. Quickly picking up speed, me steering and Andy holding on at the back, we raced down the road, instead of the path. If a car had been coming up from around the corner, I wouldn't have been here to tell the tale, that's for sure... but no car did. As the excitement level increased, our pulses racing, hair blowing in the imagined slipstream, we were yelling and whooping with the buzz, a mixture of fun and fear. As we picked up even more speed, we both suddenly realised that there was no working brakes on the damned thing! The excitement soon turned to worry as we realised that, short of throwing ourselves off the bogey, we had to go the whole way and hope for the best with no means of stopping. The thought now entered our heads that this D.I.Y designed over-grown toy on wheels was most likely meant for back garden use only. As we neared the bottom of the hill and tried to veer right to take the swift corner, our vehicle made a sudden impact with a parked car, its left front wheel ramming home straight into the space between the body of the car and the tyre of the car's front wheel. We went flying off the contraption and landed grazed and dazed in the middle of the road.

Stunned and amazed at our escapade, we looked around and saw no one was around to have seen what had happened. We attempted to prize the bogey out of its predicament, but to no avail. A kid came round the corner and on seeing us, he starts laughing and says "Hey up thee, does tha know whose car tha's just rammed that heap of wood scrapings into?... it's the cop who lives at that house's car... ha ha ha." Oh no! Now we were in trouble. After trying to free the contraption away again, we thought of going to knock on the door and explain what had happened. We did just that, but there was no one in. Oh no! One more attempt and we were going to abandon the thing. One more attempt and it worked, it came free! Oh yes!

As we pushed it back up the hill, our pangs of fear turned to laughter as we turned the top of the road and onto safety and home.

The next time we dared to venture off on that mode of transport was to go to the Park and try driving it from the top of the park to the bottom. It was grass, no cars and should be ok to navigate. After a couple of attempts at getting going we ventured with it down to the swimming pool, where we could see some lads hanging around. As we got closer we could see that these lads were not going to be giving us a good reception. No sooner had we got within talking distance of them they started on us. As soon as we answered them back, they got a bit heavy with proper threats. One of their threats was that they would throw both of us and our shit-mobile straight into the paddling pool. True to their word (well almost) they managed one of those promises. As we sped off up the hill, the sods grabbed our much-loved and prized new form of transport and with one heave, threw it straight into the swimming pool! And that was the last we saw of that!

Kids always had bikes. It was compulsory once you got to a certain age, and you could get to where you wanted to go and back much quicker. That is if you took the time to actually learn to ride the bloody things. I already had the dreaded three wheeler bike... one at the front and two at the back... the 1970's equivalent to Del Boy's Reliant Robin, with almost as much storage space for heaps of toy soldiers or swapping session swag too. But belting up and down the street on that suddenly appeared just a bit uncool after taking a look around and seeing what some of my mates were starting to learn to ride... and we'll not mention the ill-fated bogey again shall we!

The legendary Chopper bike (or more precisely its affable cousin the Chipper) entered our lives sometime around 1973/74. On a hot summer's day, a couple of weeks after my mate Gaz Stables had whacked me and Andy Goulty over the head with a cast-solid Crescent toy pistol sending us reeling with stars in our eyes over Norman Wisdom's wall... I had my first go on a bike... and it was on a Chipper. A trial run ensued. With no instructions from any of the gang, feet firmly off the ground I set off down our side passage hell for leather. "I can ride a bike wow!" I thought... to the shouts of "Stick the brakes on Tone" from the lads watching at the gate. 'Eh! What brakes...BANG!!! I ended up wrapped around our back garden fence. I was a bit bruised and a bit scratched and a lot grazed, but hey I can now ride a bike: the only thing to learn is how to stop and get off the bloody thing and use the brakes to do so. That Chipper was not so cool anyway... I now set my sights on a Chopper bike for the following Christmas... a red Chopper bike!!

Red has always been my favourite colour. Something about it has always attracted me. Be it the red uniforms of the classic British soldier uniform of the Zulu wars, the raspberry flavoured red lollypops, the traditional red buses that were still on the go or my favourite Dinky toy car. Red is a rich and deeply attractive colour and has a hint of danger in... it's a warning sign colour too: ideal colour for my first proper bike then!

Amongst the many great Christmas prezzies over the years, including Meccano, Scalextric and even my first Castle and fort, the red Chopper bike has to be my favourite! The excitement and anticipation was building up for weeks, maybe months... as soon as I put my order in for one I suppose. The worry was that my Mum, in her traditional almost compulsive trait of doing things, would choose either the wrong colour ("They only had the pink one left Tony" haaaaaaa!!!) or even the wrong bloody bike altogether. I think my Dad was in on this one too so maybe all would turn out right on Christmas day? I lived in hope.

The famous (or infamous) Raleigh Chopper was first introduced to a nation of adventure hungry kids as long ago as 1969. It was received with great excitement from hordes of kids who had spent all their time bent forward over the classic Raleigh racers, ending up with seemingly permanent arched back problems. You know those fellas you see walking around looking as though they are hunting for lost change or fag butts on the floor...? Well they're not; they rode their racers too much as young 'uns. Designed to emulate a shape not unlike an American dragster and a kid's world kind of homage to Dennis Hopper in 'Easy Rider', the bike had an overlong slim seat that was amply sized enough to give backies, though the instructions on the brand new bike would state 'This bicycle is not constructed to carry passengers'... this Hot Rod (potentially) bollocks-knackering-placed gear stick section bike with a penny farthing-sized back wheel sold over two million from 1970 onwards. They say - in those useless invisible surveys - that thousands of kids may have had their virility impaired from the strangely placed gear stick. The Chopper was controversial and calls for its banning were frequent, but during the 70's it was the icon of style for all kids. It was unique, exciting, dangerous and fun... us loved it and I still do... it was and is a legend!!!

Don't ask me what else I received for Christmas 1975? Probably some boxed games (I know I had 'Planet of the Apes', 'War of the Daleks' and 'Escape from Colditz' around this time, but all remained in their boxes, barely touched in favour of a two-wheeled wonder). All I can say is when I came downstairs that Christmas day, after opening up all my other prezzies, and I saw a large shape in a cardboard box with two tyres popping out of the bottom and giving off a smell of brand new rubber... WOW!!!! I've got a Raleigh Chopper... nothing else mattered! Quick let's open up the packaging and check the colour! WOW!!! It's a blinkin' red one too. They got it right. No substitutes, no 'sold out we owe you' notes... a brand new bright-red Raleigh Chopper bike for Christmas... does life ever get any better than this?

That first ride on my brand new shiny red Chopper bike was pure bliss: Christmas morning and feeling on top of the world.... Kid's heaven! I think a fair few of the lads I knew got one as well, but don't ask me the colours of theirs. The traditional Christmas ritual was still intact and here were our Dave 'n Steve coming up riding like mad up the street on their own new Chipper bikes. They didn't even get to our gate before one of 'em was broken! Our Paul (their Dad) was not amused; he always meant well and got 'em something good for Christmas and lo and behold it nearly always got broken almost straight away... but nothing deterred us all, one Chipper to fix and backies on my Chopper till it gets sorted.

Now I don't know what it was that made us all feel the strong urge to customise our much-loved Choppers as much as we did? The bike was cool as heck anyway... but Christmas would have hardly passed before I started to look at ways to add gadgets and the like to the bike. First it was a dynamo, then an extra light on the front (to complement the back light)... then more expressive and often motorbike-influenced appliances would appear. At one bit I managed to fix a make-do motorcycle fairing around the forward part of the chassis... taking those corners with knee centimetres from scraping the floor was now that bit extra exciting and a visual buzz too.

Then came the stickers all over the bike... football stickers, favourite numbers (mine being number seven, Barry Sheene's number)... and also reflectors, extra mirrors (almost echoing the classic Mod scooter), water bottle carriers, speedometer, lollypop stick in the spokes to make it sound like a real bike and so on. The Chopper bike was wrongly accused of being a human death trap, but it was a well decorated and exciting one and I can't imagine a childhood without one; it was the best thing I ever had as a kid and if I could have taken it to bed with me I would have done so. Now I had the bike the next step was to get some decent improvised race tracks set up.

I was obsessed with Grand Prix and also Barry Sheene and motorbike racing. Having never succeeded in recreating Brands Hatch - or any other decent race track replica for that matter - with the Scalextric, now was the time to set our own version up in kids' reality. Our gang's first attempt was merely a small stretch of path with a little corner roundabout with a grass verge encircled at each end of the bottom of our street. It did the job for a while and, apart from the odd adult passing us, we were left mostly undisturbed to conduct our race on what we nick-named 'Little Brands Hatch': even the Chippers were welcomed and were safe to race with us on this one. So off we would go 'hell for leather' on our bikes, usually around five or six of us around 'Little Brands Hatch'. The Chippers were given a start ahead of the Choppers and commentary was by anyone who was hanging around at the time minus a bike. Fun was a plenty, accidents, bar a few scraped legs, were far and few between and no-one fell out. We were well-behaved kids racing our bikes and well out of trouble for once.

The excitement was bound to eventually decrease: watching the older lads zooming up and down the roads on their 350 cc Suzuki's and Kawasaki's was too influential. We would hang around these older lads at the end of the street, catching up on their bike knowledge and cadging a backie every now and again off one of 'em. It was exciting and it managed to push me and Andy even further into all things motorbikes. We copied their wheelies, set up ramps to ride up and we started buying Motorcycle News, a lot of its contents going straight over our heads. I even started collecting the 'On two Wheels' motorbike collection and getting a binder or two's worth of them. Later on, when music completely took over my life, a school mate of mine came and bought all of my 'On two wheels' and MCN's for a good price. He never paid up for 'em though. That kid later got done for armed robbery some years later. I always got on with him though and didn't let a non-payment of a sale get between us... though he did always promise that he would be calling with the money for them every time I asked him. The armed robbery was not to blame in part payment needed for my motorbike mags... I don't think!

Me and Andy would also start to ask where the older lads got all of their bike stuff from and the fab stickers on their helmets and patches on their leathers etc: so in no time at all, us two could be seen browsing around Havenhand cycles and accessories, which originally used to be where the new Rotherham library got built, and later on moved to Westgate up the road. While blokes would be coming in and buying proper bike stuff, we were buying Suzuki, Kawasaki and the two Barry's' associated patches for our denim jackets. The two Barry's being Barry Sheene and Barry Ditchburn... our favourite bike racers. One of those older lads who was always a bit of a loose cannon, ok a carefree nutcase I suppose, well he ended up serving time for murder in later years. Who'd have thought it?

So, influenced by the older lads and their 350's (and the occasional 500cc), we began to look at creating a much more exciting and grittier race track. But, not satisfied with one, we opted to create two new ones, so along with the occasional bout round 'Little Brands', we now had a selection of three racetracks... Track number two was the speedway! This was a real treat and, for some reason, always took place on a Thursday evening... don't ask me why! It was a massive bullring shaped circle of a road set around a large playing area of grass just off a place called Mallory Avenue. It was set on a hill so when you went speeding around the bottom corners, you really did ride at a 45 degree angle with your back wheel almost facing flat straight behind you, just like a real Speedway. The actual road was really gritty too: just perfect.

Casualties and injuries on this track were more common-place and blood-soaked legs and even the occasional head injury would be on the agenda. It was dead exciting and great fun though. After the races it would be time to go home, read the back pages of the Rotherham Record free paper to see if any kids were flogging owt good (I never managed to buy anything out of there, and knew no one else who did... the only time I rang up from a phone box one day with some spare pennies, was for some extra Scalextric track and some bastard had beat me to it.) Wolfing down some of Mother's home-made Blackberry Pie and the traditional Top of the Pops would have to do. Top of the Pops followed the home of futuristic scientific wonder 'Tomorrow's World' which we would watch half-interested, half in awe at the prospects of the inventions and creations that were awaiting us in the 1980's. For now, though, life was still simple for us kids, and Thursdays and bike-riding and bike-racing were great.

The third and last race track was our respectfully named Daytona 3000. The older lads would race good and proper around this road, which stretched a good half mile or so around a whole block, which included part of a bus route and a seriously dangerous and tempting long and fast hill down Hague Avenue. We would watch the bikes start off from the bottom of our street and race around there so we had to have a go ourselves too. How we didn't kill ourselves on this race I will never know. We reached some serious speeds and rode as reckless and unheeding of any danger whatsoever as we could... we had heroes to live up to after all.

One day, on this route, but not on an actual race, me and a mate called Ian Cooper (a great lad who I always got on with and never fell out with once)... well we were riding our bikes down this route. I was being all big-headed and shouting to Ian about how we would race around this road. My front wheel was swerving from side to side and my speed was picking up deliberately, as if to emphasise how care-free and brave I was. I was laughing and loving it and Ian was looking a bit worried... Faster and faster I rode: next thing over I went, straight over the handle bars and onto the middle of the road with my Chopper bike following me and wrapping itself all around me as if it comprised of a hundred grasping tentacles all desperate to catch me in their grasp... wheel spokes, bike chain and brake wires all became part of my being as I skidded and slid down the road, incapable of halting my descent... this was a busy road at times and if a vehicle had been coming either way, I would have been in serous trouble. I ended up a crumpled heap of flared jeans, aggressively torn t-shirt and bike-greased hair complete with grazes and cuts more visible than the colour of my skin. Ian slammed his breaks on and stopped to my aid. I was in shock. Looking around, an old flat-cap wearing fella, who we knew as a miserable cantankerous old git was passing - walking stick in hand - and took one look at me and said something along the lines of "What tha bloody doin' int middle of road, yer soft apeth"... and in, most likely some comparison to his experiences in the Boer War, finished off with "Get thee sen up or tha'll get thee sen killed laying theer like that." "Umm no sympathy coming from that corner then", I remember thinking at the time. "I think its time to go 'ome and get me tea don't you Ian", I said and buggered off home dragging my beloved red chopper bike along with me.

Life's full of lessons and that was one that I learnt the hard way when I was a kid. There were plenty more to learn as time went on, but for now that one was well enough for me. The accident didn't put me off bike-riding, and I didn't blame my chopper for it either. It was business as usual for us and our bikes, but I was certainly gonna go a bit more careful in future, that's for sure... well for at least a few days at least!

Adventures that followed included a superb real dirt track that cut through a soon-to-be developed for houses area of land and was a real bump of a ride. It was wide enough for just one bike so we followed each other down. As we hit a certain point about halfway down, where the track dipped all of a sudden, we went right through the air for a few split seconds: what a buzz that was! Of course the houses got built and that was the end of that one as homes began to replace kid's playgrounds.

One day on a bike ride when we ventured to the edges of Wentworth we were suddenly engulfed, as if from nowhere, by a thirty-strong gang of leather jacket-wearing, long-haired and tough-looking bunch of bike riders.... Greasers on bicycles. They were on us like a swarm of bees, blocking our way and intimidating us. They looked mean as hell and meaning business. It was a new feeling for me, and most likely the rest of us, this. We had scrapped and fought with each other and other kids that we knew, but never come across a gang like this one. Marlon Brando in The Wild One would have recruited 'em, I am confident. I think it was our Dave who they spotted wearing his Rotherham Utd scarf and they weren't impressed one bit. The fear in our faces must have been so clear to see. "How the heck are we gonna get out of this one", I remember thinking. Not only are we seriously out-numbered and well out of our league here, but they are also obviously not Rotherham fans; not by any stretch of the imagination.

Tugging and pulling at us and booting our bikes, the gang continued to hound and intimidate us. There were quite a few tears starting to well up within our pitiful little bunch of bike riders: no way were we nice little do-gooder Scouts material and could hold our own if need be in a fair scrap, but not against these older fully-recruited tough 'uns. If we could have retreated like bleedin' cowards we would have done so, no hesitation. One of the big 'uns spurred on, no doubt, by his army of lower ranks, started to focus on our Rotherham Utd scarves. I remember coming up with the daft idea of saying that we didn't support Rotherham (sorry Millers!) and that we had only just found all the scarves on our bike trek. It would never work I thought, but no harm in trying. As one of the lads was just starting to try and drag our Dave off of his bike, I told them the Judas-like deed. "We weren't proper Rotherham fans." "It will never deter 'em, this surely...???" It bloody well did! With a few more choice words and lapping up of their superiority, the gang all laughed at us and turned away and rode off! A notch on their chart of toughness and a kick in the balls for ours... but one point for evading a good hiding (what is a good hiding anyway... I would think that any person receiving one would not agree in calling it a good hiding?). This tactic of sussing a situation out and making the right move could and would prove to be very helpful in years to come when surrounded by glued-up aggressive skinheads and the like. For now, though, we had survived to live another day. That was my first bike ride out of Rawmarsh - our base - and I never did like greasers after that day!

Chapter Six

Mischievous times

"I was always mischievous and I am told I still am. I can't stand being bored and hate to see everything being set up and taken seriously without the slightest hint of humour involved. When people get pious and self-righteous and up on their high horse about something, I always want to do something to upset the apple cart. I just can't help it, it's the way I am and it's got me into trouble quite a few times."

I always wanted to have a joke and lark around. I got restless when there was no fun being had. During my school days my teachers were constantly having words with my parents saying I was ok for a while and would start off concentrating on the work at hand, but would always eventually become bored and restless and then take it upon myself to have a wander around the classroom and see what the other kids were up to, often distracting them and spoiling their concentration. Kids would ask me to not go near 'em so I didn't make them laugh and get them into trouble: It's true, I am to blame... I couldn't help it. It was fun!

Nowadays the do-gooders would insist I needed rehabilitative therapy or something: back then I simply got done! If a teacher got me done, I would take their punishment, usually the slipper on the backside, but would make sure that they knew it did not bother me. Their weapon was a slipper, mine was defiance!

At this point, you may well ask "Did I really intensely dislike my teachers?" ... well the truth is, mostly, no! I don't reckon I truly and deeply hated any of them at all, though I did come close to it at times and can say that I did severely dislike one or two of 'em. So why did I so object to doing what my teachers told me instead of simply knuckling down and getting my work done? At the time, I don't think I truly understood why that was; it was more of an urge to do the opposite of what they had in mind for me, or often, me being just plain old bored and having a low attention span. I also had a growing dislike for authority and being told what to do, so to combine all of these ingredients together I had the makings of a fledgling small-village school rebel. Nowt like some kids, though. Blimey, one lad I knew booted the hell out of the teachers back at the infants. I can remember walking past him and being open-mouthed and amazed at seeing him being held and restrained by two teachers who were trying to calm him down and all the while he was laying the boot in and spitting at them. He had some serious issues going on, that's for sure, and made my cottage-industry school rebellion seem like a script from Trumpton!

But, my agendas were not so much of an angry stance – that would come quite some time later on – mine were more born of frustration and, if I am gonna be perfectly honest, more than an average dose of insecurity. Regardless of all of this, my natural leaning towards wanting to have a good laugh and disrupt seriousness would get me into trouble anyway.

The actual teachers could be ok, I suppose, in their own ways. Well, some of them. They did have a lot to deal with, we were gits to start with and the classes were a lot bigger back then, or so they seemed. I reckon there would have been an average of maybe over 30 kids in each of our lessons, so it can't have been easy to deal with. Amongst those kids would be a mixture of swots who would so easily pick up on what was being taught without complaint or a hint of disagreement, slow kids who needed extra attention and repeated instructions, lazy kids, annoying kids, boring kids, thieving kids, liars, trouble causers and nutters. Some teachers had a slight sense of humour, most did not. Most nutters had an erratic sense of humour and little misgivings at giving the teachers some lip and taking the punishment when dished out. At least a small handful of kids I knew (but maybe didn't knock around with all of the time) were like that and would develop a serious extension of that attitude and, in later life, push it right to the very limit and go all the way to prison! So, teachers... you weren't so bad off trying to teach me after all!

Away from the restrictions of school, more fun could be had, as long as someone was willing to join in, that is. Arriving home after a hard day's work (er umm) at school to the kids' TV delights of 'King Arthur and the Britons', 'Time Slip' or the Tomorrow People (what exactly was that kids' show all about?) and a jam sandwich for tea, weather permitting, it was a choice of what to do, who to call for and where to go... and don't forget to leave those knitting needles of me Mothers that she had left lying around, stuck up on the settee for someone to sit on... ouch!!!

It's a myth, a cliché and quite possibly a downright wishful thinking over-emphasised heck of a lie, but all the same I will state it once more... the sun always seemed to be shining for us kids back in the seventies. The fifties had been grey – I am assured of that with evidence to support the theory – the sixties were an explosive wave of psychedelic Technicolor as everyone woke up from the miserable war-inflicted rationed fifties to realise that the world was their oyster, sex was fun and the rock n' roll rebellion had not been a flash in the pan. Now the seventies still had colour, and much longer hair than before: and the clothes were in many cases absolutely atrocious till Punk kicked in (and many would debate the worth of that fashion's look too)... but for us kids, the seventies were sunny, lots of fun and exciting... end of story!

It was during these sunny days that we had a hell of a lot of our fun. Hours of outdoor games from hide n' seek (with kids scarpering through the long over-grown back gardens non-stop on long summer evenings), Kerby, window-smashing cricket on the street to football on the street or when the caretaker wasn't looking... the school field. Also, our military campaigns, either in life-sized involvement – if enough kids were willing to join in and risk getting belted by a hard plastic rifle if caught by the enemy

... or our long-standing battles with our mini-sized soldier regiments (that often ended up reconnoitring down the street)... hell there was plenty to do during these red-hot summer days... that is until every game had been exhausted and it all became unexciting: and that's when, predictably, the mischief started!

Of course, lads being lads, there would be scraps now and again with each other. Someone would say something out of hand and things would kick off. One particular row between us ended when a kid on a bike passed by down the street and ran over poor old Gary Mitchell. The rest of us stood watching as time seemed to stand still and we watched him going round with, first the front wheel of the bicycle, and then the back wheel: we could see his face looking at us as it went round looking as though it was permanently attached to the wheel and saying "What's happening to me?"

Another time, this kid who had been taking the mickey out of us non-stop for weeks, if not months, finally came into our grasp: as he came down our street on his bike, I managed to catch him and after telling him what my problem was, punched him and pushed him straight off his bike and onto the road: no there was no car coming, they were every ten minutes on a busy day back then. After another thump in the gob I left him to it, but his Dad appeared out of nowhere and he blubbered his story to him. When the kid's Dad heard what I had to say and what he had been saying about us, and especially what I told him that he had said about him (lying of course) well he got another clip round the lughole too!

Taking the piss out of people was fun, until you got caught and had to suffer a damned good pasting... That was the rule of the land. We dished it out if they weren't too big to have some good odds against, and when we got cornered we had to take it back. It's a good job we were good at getting away, though, otherwise we would have been permanently getting a hiding off of someone. On the way to school, one day, me and Pete Roddis were in hysterics at the almost Dinky-sized Charm Carpets van. Pointing and laughing at the driver, he got out shaking his fists at us and saying it wasn't a toy he was driving, along with a few polite words thrown in. One day a certain John Harrison caught some of us out of our territory and him being an ardent Leeds fan and hearing that we were Rotherham fans and had been laughing at Leeds fans, started to push us around and give us some lip... him and his mate chased us all over Rawmarsh and then gave each of us a thump for our persistence. Some years later (in a Punk V Mod scrap) the lad got some fist back off my mate Pete and that made things even... in a way and then we became great friends... me and John.

We must have had names for everyone that we knew existed and saw on a regular basis: most of these would not take great offence but when the names got far too cruel then the trouble could start. The old fella at the bottom of the street threatened to 'cut our 'eads off' with a scythe after we had started mimicking his poor goofy wife and she daren't walk past us without receiving a hail of mimicry, the bastards we were!

One day we did go a bit too far when we lifted a hefty boulder-sized piece of rock and placed it right in the middle of the road knowing that one of our favourite tormenting receivers would be veering around the corner from work at 5.15pm. His Reliant Robin would have been minus another wheel or worse had he not spotted the middle of the road obstruction. He got out and managed to move it aside and must have known it was our doing, but he never said a word. Maybe he didn't fancy any reprisals? Nowadays we would certainly attain a ASBO for that or maybe some time in a young offenders institution... back then kids were kids and we got away with most of it... WHY? cos we hardly ever got caught. Tricks were a part of my life and I couldn't resist partaking in them, it gives some fun to things and a good laugh. I still continued the tradition throughout my 1970's coming of age journey and beyond. Like the time, some years later, when my Mum first got her bus pass. She had to fix a photo in there to show the bus driver each time she got on the bus, so I put a photo of a monkey-looking caveman in there without her knowing. In perfect jest it worked and the next day she opened up her bus pass with the primeval being gazing the drivers' way. Mum was totally oblivious until the driver made a comment of something along the lines of "Is that a recent photo of you there then?"

Then there was the time our Glen was going mad for the last slice of jam and cream cake that was mine that I had saved while everyone else had eaten theirs. He was going mad for it and I kept tormenting him saying "No, I am having it when I fancy it." Eventually, an idea sprung to mind and I offered it to him saying "Go on then, you can have it," laughing as he shot into the pantry for his cake fix. He came through with it, took a good hefty bite into it and spat it out saying "You rotten little sod, you've put tomato ketchup in it." My belly was aching with laughter. Maybe he did get his own back when he threw me across the room, another day, and I landed with my foot stuck in the electric fire, which (luckily for me) wasn't switched on at the time: Some you win, some you lose!

One mischievous escapade that we did get caught doing, though, was while playing Olympic javelin with the Golf course flag poles. We were out on one of our after-school jaunts in the local park (Rosehill Park and also known as Victoria Park) and had made our way to the popular mini Golf course that used to be there back then. What could we do for some fun, was the question? Rawmarsh illegal Olympics story coming up soon.

Victoria Park was opened at Rosehill in Rawmarsh in 1901, often being referred to as Rosehill Park too. The hall within its grounds was built in 1830 by the Firth family and was acquired, along with the grounds, by the local council in honour of Queen Victoria's Diamond Jubilee of 1897. Throughout the years the park has been a great source of enjoyment for generations of children, courting couples and families, though, sometimes hitting low peaks and an ill reputation for safety. A magnet for youths throughout the years, petty mischief and somewhere to socialise often being the true reasons for their congregating. Back in the 1970's, however, the climate of any potential drug-taking-mugging gangs of youths was far away on the horizon! Even so, there was one incident of a kid being seriously assaulted by an older kid in the park. The rumour quickly went around that someone was on the loose trying to cut kid's dicks off, which made us cringe, scared and for a while wear an extra pair of Y-Fronts.

....

The mid 70's would soon be the late 70's. Time was moving on, but not too fast. Each year and its experiences had their own space and time. Blimey, a Japanese soldier even appeared out of the jungle for the first time since WW2, not knowing the war was over it was reported on the news, which I thought was hilarious. In the meantime, we had to enjoy what was left of the decade... we were almost halfway through it by now but the thought of 1984 and the futuristic 1980's seemed a lifetime away. As we changed our school years and each of my school reports got progressively worse (but not quite bad enough to warrant any serious action being taken against me) I began to experience new and so far to me, undiscovered fads... watching horror films on my own late on Friday nights ('The Wicker man', 'Dracula', 'Frankenstein' and 'The Mummy' not seeming quite as scary as a few years back, though Peter Cushing did manage to send a shiver down my spine.) Oh and the gorgeous Susan George in anti-babysitting advertising vehicle 'Fright.' The other new pastime was Gum card collecting. Stevie next door gave me his Battle cards... these were actually banned at one point for being too graphic in their portrayal of World war two)... and that set me off with yet another obsession!

A selection of the notorious Battle gum cards we collected, these being some of the tamer ones available

Other cards that joined this new collecting bug were 'Planet of the Apes', 'The High Chaparral', 'Batman', a pop music series (I got a really cool David Bowie as Ziggy Stardust one) and a heap of footie ones, where I aimed to learn as many footie players as I could, from Alan Ball to Peter Osgood. Gum cards were really popular with kids in the playground and we all lapped 'em up. The packs usually had four or five cards of a particular theme and a stick of rock-hard bubbly gum. On the back would be either some story relating to the front theme or form part of a jigsaw of a larger picture that completes with you finishing the whole collection... a con into pushing you further ahead in searching for that card with Urko's nose on! Gum cards were great: they were colourful and enticing and the packets smelt lovely too cos of the bubblegum inside. They lasted a short time in most kid's interest rates and were soon overtaken by some other fad... or yet more mischievousness!

I mentioned, just a bit earlier, the local park's javelin match. Now we had all seen Spartacus and all the other Roman, Gladiator and Medieval Knights films that involved spear throwing and the like. It so happens, also, that Rosehill Park's Golf course, not being used at that precise moment, was an ideal setting for our own version of the Greek Olympics... the javelin contest in particular! Wow, wouldn't it be a great idea to find out who was the best at lunging a well aimed spear over at the passing cars and see who gives the best performance. Well, none of us were good enough to manage that, and I reckon, between us, we may have realised that the deed may have been one act of naughtiness too far. We settled for a simple 'see how far we can throw the javelin contest' instead.

There was me, our Dave, best mate Andy and future Cockney Rejects fan Ricky. I think there may have been one of the other lads there too, but time has eroded my memory as to whom it was? If it was you, you don't have to own up! Anyway we were having a grand old time of it, practising our skills at imagining impaling a Barbarian warrior to the old oak tree at the edge of the park. We weren't too bad a team at this, but just as I was launching my next stab a jam sandwich comes speeding around the corner of the park screeching to a halt at the sight of the unofficial Olympics of 1974.

I can see the two cops now: leaping out of the doors of their punishment wagon, all arms flailing and legs sprinting right into our domain. The heart was thumping and the adrenalin was speeding like an express train: "chuffin' hell the cops are after us" we shouted. We dispersed each and every way possible. There was only four (maybe five) of us, but looking around as I contemplated which way to make my escape... it looked as though we were a whole regiment of trapped prisoners of war wishing to make their unanticipated escape route. Each of us scarpered... me and Andy shot straight across the park 45 degrees parallel to the cops' direction. We ran like we had never run before. At the edge of the park we zoomed straight across the road, never even glancing if there was any traffic in our way... there wasn't and we survived – heads down and making our escape.

Next we leaped over the bushes and wild woodland debris into the midst of an area we had not ventured before. Straight down the hillside we slid, sweat dripping off of us and bush hats bouncing off our heads, grazing our legs, arms and backsides, we managed to come to a halt around half-way down this seemingly endless slope of naturalist oblivion. Grabbing a hold of some branches to halt our descent, we both regained our positioning and looked round for a suitable hiding place. "We have had it this time" we remarked to each other; surely we will end up behind bars now. What were our parents gonna say... tears in our eyes and worry etched across our faces we laid down, stayed motionless and waited while the cops managed to locate us. It seemed like forever that half hour or so... we eventually got the guts to try and climb a bit further back up the hill and try and listen to what was going off over at the park. We couldn't hear owt so continued to scale the heights of Monte Cassino and see if we could see what we couldn't hear. When we got to the top the scene had reached its conclusion and there was no one to be seen. Most importantly, the cops were gone.

When we got back to base, we caught up with the others. It transpired that the cops had caught them and they had owned up to everything and gave 'em their names etc. They said that the cops were still after us. Maybe, we thought, they had told 'em that the whole thing had been down to us? I dunno, we never got caught and escaped all notions of punishment and reproach. Our parents never found out either... so I suppose yet again we didn't actually get caught: but this was far too close for our liking.

Around this time, our Paul and Glen took me and our Dave to our first football matches to see Rotherham Utd at Millmoor. I can remember being amazed how big the pitch was compared to Saturday night's 'Match of the Day' ones. The noise was louder than our Rediffusion telly too and the language was slightly more varied and colourful than the BBC commentator's chit chat. Our Glen dressed me up in a Rotherham scarf, hat and one of them clackers or whatever they were called. When we got there, after passing a load of lads scrapping with each other, I noticed future

Punk and Mod face Zal in there amongst them (He was a Blades fan so either Rotherham were playing Sheff Utd or he was there just for the scrap?). We then went to the visitors end and to my amazement there was a train line running straight behind the back of the football ground. Over at the Kop end at another match me and our Dave were placed up on the top of the wall right at the back/top of the Kop. While we were sat up there, our Dave poured a cup of Bovril over a bloke's head just below us. It's a good job it weren't red-hot! Talk about football hooliganism... difference is that we picked our own fans to practise on. the bloke went mad looking all over the show for the culprit and me and our Dave just carried on watching the match.

These matches never really caught my imagination, being yet another quick phase of interest, and after the initial excitement of the first few, I started to lose interest. If I never took a proper serious involvement in following football religiously, preferring to have a knock about with me mates rather than watch it, then my initiation to live footie with Rotherham Utd may be to blame: not long afterwards I went through a phase of supporting Liverpool as many lads did back then due to their providence and star player- Kevin Keegan. Eventually I lost interest altogether and ultimately only one pastime kept me truly interested in life.

Summertime held lots of opportunities for general mischievous activities. Me, our Dave and Steve had a great little den at the back of their garden and there we would plan out what to get up to. If no good ideas were suggested, we could always climb the trees in the corner which overlooked the lounge of the Monkwood Hotel pub. Climbing to the top of the trees with a bag of crab apples we would belt the hell out of the windows with our missiles and laugh at the outraged faces shaking their fists at us, spilling their pints of beer all over the place. I wonder were they Tetley bitter men?

In that pub's back garden was a wooden shed that sold crisps in the summer. I would see my future pal John Harrison constantly eyeing the shed up. One day the shed was raided and emptied of just about all of its crisps, sweets and snacks. Years later, when me and him were drinking patrons of the pub John owned up to the act and admitted it was him and a mate who had stripped it of all of its edibles. They had a great summer and never went hungry on nights out roaming the streets.

Summer seemed to never end and the fun likewise. Around this time, two fab periods of lads' adventure came into being with the invention of two full-on in yer face battle games we came up with. First off, whilst roaming further away than our local streets, we came across a place just pleading to be played around at. Its land was being re-designed and excavated. Whilst doing this, the people in their diggers and over-sized Tonka toys had left an area to be completed at a later date, basically a slice of land looking like something from a war film, quarry-like with cliffs and rocks and rubble and every other detail a kid might want to recreate those action scenes seen whilst watching Robert Mitchum in 'Anzio' on the telly. We named it the corral and ventured up there every single day after school... 4pm till almost dark. There was me, Andy Goulty, our Dave and Steve, I think Gary Mitchell and around six or seven other lads we had recruited.

Right from getting there we set up our armies. We had brought our plastic rifles and accoutrements along too, but our main ammo was lying around all over the place, great big chunks of hard clay that made fantastic missiles and make-do grenades! So, starting at one end of the cliff edge to the other we disappeared into our own platoons ready for battle. The battle would commence and an all-out assault would begin with an endless attack of clay bricks and stones being fired from each cliff at the enemy. You could hear the ouches and "bloody 'eck that hurt" as the missiles hit their targets and you could feel the impact, yourself, of being hit smack-bang at the side of the head with one of these cannon balls... and it did bloody hurt too, but not quite enough for anyone to get seriously hurt, we believed.

On a typical battle there, the first ten minute salvo would then be followed by a full-frontal attack by one side while the defence line of the other would lie in wait for the enemy to get closer. Peering over the edge of the clay cliff, we would wait until the kids got closer and then open up on them. Kids would be falling down, dropping their weapons and ammo and trying to cover their heads in protection. If the defence had been strong enough to hold off the attack, then we would all dive down the slippery slope and give them chase. This could go on for hours, along with diversionary tactics and moments of quiet when some of us would patrol out on a spying mission to see what the others were up to, usually catching them chewing on Curly Wurlys' and sucking Spangles and liquorice. These battles were real good stuff and the excitement levels were up and beyond any before.

For a two to three week period we all felt like we were escaping into another world; miles away from the routine of school and home. It was just like being a part of a real war. Nowadays, you could compare it to an activity such as Paintball, but ours was nowhere near as safe. The fun was brought to a halt one day by chance. When we were on our way over the land making our way back to the gates and across the road home, we saw a Digger shovelling the coal and slag away and when it stopped the driver got out and walked towards us. When he reached us (we decided not to run as the gate was beyond him and also we, naively, didn't think we were doing anything wrong), he looked us all up and down and giving us a smile went in his pocket and shared out a handful of change for us all to have, saying "Go on kids, get to the shop and get some sweets, but don't come back on here anymore as its not safe." "Fair enough" we thought, "At least we haven't got proper done and we have come away with some spog money too. Not so sure we should not bother coming back though, its too much fun."

When we got home, one of us let it out to one of our parents about a stranger giving us some money to buy some sweets. Alarm bells started ringing for our collective guardians and we got the classic line of "We have told you time and time again, never accept anything from strangers" which was fair enough but we weren't going to turn down free sweets were we? As our adventures of the last few weeks began to unfold on adult ears more alarm bells started ringing. On finding out where we had been playing, we were all giving a right proper ticking off and forced to promise that we would never go there again. It turns out we had been playing on a daily basis on an extremely dangerous work site and the cliffs we had used as our battlefield could have collapsed at any given moment covering, possibly fatally, any of us beneath a mountain of clay. When you look back at this, you realise the danger and depth, but to us kids it was our action paradise and after all none of us got anything more severe than a few bruises and cuts. But so ended the campaigns at the O' Clay Corral!

Following this adventure, not long after, we decided to start going on walks further afield, where adults wouldn't know what we were up to at all. The Tarzan rope up Manor Farm was a pull for a while, as was the Valley, where kids entered their own theme park of fun, games, fights and mayhem in a scenic and nature-filled environment. Yet again, the mean grown ups that controlled our surroundings proved their spiteful nature and flattened the Valley. We started going down the bridle path, which was an old Roman built cobbled path on a hill down the back of civilisation as we knew it.

On the way there, one time, the gang of us decided to pay a visit into the old abandoned Church on Chapel Walk. Upon entering, we had a good old nosy around the place before daring each other to go down into the basement. We had heard that the Church was supposed to be haunted so this dare gave an extra bite to it. We went down the hole and down some old brick stairs and turning the corner took the plunge and, one by one, stepped into the abyss of the basement. Never so far had I known such darkness as that basement. You could not see one single thing. It was cold, smelt of old masonry and just old oldness. It was also deathly quiet and well creepy. Sending nervous shivers down our spines we stayed there for all of half a minute or so, no one daring to be the first to say "Let's go." Then, stood around, not being able to see each other or know exactly where we were standing and what was beneath or in front of us, it came ... "Oooooorrrrr..... Oooooorrrrr" the sounds of a moaning Ghost. "Ooooooorrr Ooooorrrrrr" "Crap... get piggin' out of here" our Dave shouted and we all turned around falling all over in the darkness, ending up knocking each of us down and clambering as one up the stairs of hell and out into the peace of the top layer of churchly heaven. Collecting ourselves outside, we all started laughing, scared it is true, but excited... was that a real ghost noise we all thought? I asked myself too, was it? Was it eckers like a bloody real Ghost, it was either one of us lot mimicking the sound (no-one owned up to it though) or some other kid down there awaiting a gang of pillocks such as us passing by for a nosy. Or maybe an old tramp waking up? Years later, our Glen was working on the demolition of that church and he found an old bottle with an issue of the Advertiser paper in it from the 1800's that had been buried for the future. He never saw or heard of any Ghosts being captured or spotted, though.

Our destination after that was to follow the old Roman Bridle Path and make a right turn to a long tree-lined walker's path that, half way along, had a decent stream close to it. When we got there, we started our new game, which was basically our old game that we had been playing up at the Corral, except this was done from each side of the stream and involved hanging off the branches of trees to attack your enemy and trying to get across the stream without getting wet. You see the objective of this improvised venture was to get the enemy as wet-through soaked as was humanly possible by flinging logs, bricks and anything at hand nearest to where they were. Now that good old game was a great laugh and became our new adventure for some weeks to come. Trouble is, we never got offered any sweets from anyone!

Summer interests also took in collecting bird's eggs: little did we realise how cruel a hobby that was, though we did sense that it was not quite right, but not really sure why! We would call for each other to go nesting. Finding bird's nests in bushes and trees and the like we would carefully get in there, usually getting scratched to heck with thorns, and gently nick a couple of eggs. They would be very carefully placed into a shoe-box with cotton wool cushioning in and the lid put on, taken back to their hiding place: mine was in the out-house, not exactly a safe place really.

Either when the eggs were straight away found, or when brought home, the trick would be to then gently tap a hole at the top and bottom of the egg and after giving it a gentle shake, blow through the top hole so that the egg's contents would stream out of the bottom hole. Were these fertilised embryos or just egg yolk? At our ages we never really gave it much deep thought. There were different names and status of rank for all the different types of eggs and kids would have to jealously guard their collections as they could often be up for nicking. If some other lads out there knew that you had a particular rare egg, they would offer to swap for five common ones: if they didn't manage to coax it from you that way, the obsession could lead to 'em attempting to swipe it, or threaten to beat you up for it. Some kids' collections also got smashed out of jealousy or rivalry. I would wonder, a few years later, what effect we had on the course of nature?

Swapping bird's eggs wasn't the only tradition of trying to get the best bargain from what yer mates had. Me and Andy Goulty re-launched our regular Sunday afternoon swapping session fad. It had all started with a few toys to swap and before you knew it we were swapping unwanted soldiers (unreliable cowards, misfits and unwilling to heal ones being the first to walk the swapping plank) and also gum cards, comics, board games, Subbuteo players, tennis rackets and Corgi vehicles. Being joined by any kid we warranted had owt we thought may be interesting, we would set up on Andy's front lawn and charge only a two and a half pence mix up to join in with the swapping mania: no kid we laughed at was allowed though and I bet they were bloody well glad too! Sometimes a little scrap would break out over someone bragging that they had got the best bargain or something: me and Andy, even though we were in charge of the events, would also still fall out some of the time and grown ups would pass by pointing at these two kids with half of their toy collections spread across the front lawn trying to knock the hell out of each other. I am sure that's when some of our stuff got swiped, and this could well be the cause of an unsettled squabble the next time. "Well you nicked my table tennis bat when I weren't looking". "No I dint, its crap anyway and it's bent too"... meanwhile Suckabogey was riding up the street with a smashing new table tennis bat.

....

There were some right old characters knocking about during our days of growing up... some of them, you just knew were legends, and deservedly too. Jockey Gee for example. Never a nicer man you should come to meet. Jockey Gee was a real classic character. He had a history of supposedly being in the RAF for about three days, being a removal man with a wheel barrow ("Any job taken, none too small" was his motto... and many a newly housed family must have taken out business with the gent) and he was also a very funny man too... could he tell a tale? Not bloomin' half!

Jockey Gee was a part of a generation whose glory days had passed well before our 1970's sun-soaked days: their generation being a time of National service, prefabs, boozers for men only and everyone knew who their neighbour and who the next estate's neighbour was. I liked Jockey Gee, he made us laugh, and he never had a bad word to say about anybody and a ready smile for all. When greeted with his opening lines of "Hey up me little petal, how are yer then me little fruitcake" how could you not smile ... Jockey Gee once passed me and Andy when we were sat on our wall and upon us saying "Hey up, here comes Jockey Gee"... both of us laughing, he laughed too and gave us a nice little gentle push straight over the hedge: we were laughing as we collided going over and landing on the lawn we immediately both knew that we had just been given a classic episode to re-tell and laugh at in future days to come. The world of Jockey Gee had passed us by and were we glad for it. Modern times are sorely missing the Jockey Gees of this world!

Other memorable characters were Vinegar Liz in the town centre, always with her dog and always hanging around Staniforths' bakers and always muttering to herself whilst in her own little insular world... the Bionic Man who was far from Bionic, though if he had ever got to carry out all of his threats on people his victims would have needed more than a re-build programme for bionic breakthrough. He was as mad as a hatter that one and if you ever got stuck with him on a bus get ready for a long journey was the reward. There was Custer (the man who walked as though he had been shot by arrows in his arm and because he had long hair too... well the name fit) and also a gang of nutters, a lot older than us lot, who used to go to a house around the corner for the lasses and get pissed up and start trouble. One day one of 'em came out and had a go at me and one of my mates, Shaun Angell, and was offering us out: I wouldn't mind but he was about ten years older than us and was as cross-eyed as Clarence the lion and would have most likely knocked himself out before us. When he was threatening us he was looking at someone in the front room of an house behind us... who was peering through going "Eh me?" Anyway Shaun would have bleeding battered him to heck... we named him 'Contro.' Ten minutes later and one of his gang emerged on a tiny push bike, pissed as a fart and rode past us going "Oh uh oh'... 'Oh uh oh'.... Oh uh oh"... sounding like a cross between Johnny Weissmuller and Jimmy Savile... did we laugh? Of course we blinkin' did... we still do to this day! The world around us was full of funny characters, crackpots and look-alikes... how could we not be having a laugh a minute within this time of our lives childhood...!

While we were growing up and having as much fun as we could, a lot of things were happening in the outside (and far bigger) world. Something called Watergate had occurred, grown ups were growing their hair yet even longer and some pop groups on the telly even wore make up. The Vietnam war was still raging too, though the USA had already began a slow withdrawal of their forces as the 70's began. One particularly vivid memory for myself, and the world over, is the photo of the poor young naked Vietnamese girl fleeing helplessly from a Napalm attack. It was the sight of real war and its effect on even kids younger than us. As I was setting my toy soldiers up on the floor that day I was affected by that. I thought war was something honourable and did not affect kids. That innocent little kid could have been me or one of my mates or the little lass across the street if we had been born at the wrong time and in the wrong place. I always remember that... the luck of the draw of life!

The great British summer may have been the ideal setting for creating trouble... But the winter was an ideal setting for proper undercover mischievousness. Knock a door run was a traditional, almost daily routine: 'bang bang bang' and off we would run... most of the time any potential pursuers would not get to their front gate before we had disappeared into the foggy night, but there was always some clever bastard out to prove himself and state very clearly that he could out-run us, out-smart us and catch us. That clever twat couldn't climb bloody trees though, so we would end up ten foot up a tree (on streets that still had trees) and laughing at the fella shaking his fists at us and throwing threats at us and shaking the tree as much as he could to loosen his prey. We took the piss, but if only he had had the patience to wait, we would have had to come down as our Mothers would have soon been shouting us in. Some adults just didn't have much common sense back then! And it's a good job for us too.

Knock a door run became a starter task on mischievous night, but tying every dustbin on the street together and then to the door knobs of each house and then knocking on a couple of doors was one step further... and absolutely hilarious too. Opening the door to our frantic front-door banging, the rope would pull and each bin would pile over and empty its contents all over the street. We would be running off laughing like mad.

The next event after mischievous night was Bonfire night or more commonly known to us lot as Bonny neet: my t'old mother called it Bumfire night!!! I was troubled for years as to whose backside was actually being set alight. Penny for the guy was compulsory, often involving one of us sat down on the floor wearing our parkas huddled right up to our necks, head down, hood up... soon to be unmasked as a fake when some passing kid would come and boot yer! The local chiropodist took exception to us penny begging near his establishment one year and removed poor old Guy's ead from his body (actually an old football) and booted it right down the hill telling us to scarper... why did a chiropodist have to be so nasty... was it the annoyance of playing with people's feet all day that did him? Anyway poor old Guy Fawkes got drawn and head-quartered yet again; Some things in human nature never change do they?

Everyone seemed to have their own Bonfire; it was a big thing Bonny neet. The week before would see squads of kids out searching for some wood, gates would be removed, old seesaws, loose fences the lot: if you had the nerve to actually build yours up the night before, then you had better provide a reliable look-out as rest assured the other gangs would be after it, and they would bloody well get it for their own as soon as yer back was turned and once taken that was the end of your Bonny neet!

The night would arrive, and on coming home from school would be the smell of cordite in the air. That cold breeze with the smell of fireworks in the air is synonymous with the night. As darkness set in Fireworks and Bonfires would be set alight! The stuff that went on those bonfires was unbelievable and the poisonous odours from plastic and other undesirable Bonny ingredients was out of hand... owt went on there and it didn't matter whose it was half the time. All you over-grown kids out there reading this. Did you ever wonder where all those toys, books, comics and other still much-loved toys went? Well they most likely went on the back-garden bonfire; if not your own, then maybe on ours. I was just a bit pissed off to be standing watching the ember of the flames one year when over my head comes flying the hefty ramparts of my much respected Fort Apache straight onto the fire. The next year's fire was welcomed with my sturdy (dungeon included) Medieval Castle as it's stabilising middle: those poor Britain's toy Knights turned dungeon prisoners really did suffer a medieval punishment... close my eyes and try and ignore the screams was the best option and look forward to the chestnuts (and their obligatory hidden maggots) to arrive on the ashes of poor Sir Galahad's funeral pyre.

Of course, no Bonfire could ever be complete without fireworks... they were the epitome of Bonfire excitement and danger. The sounds of crackers going off non-stop would sound like the Battle of El Alamein from 5pm onwards. When everyone had arrived it would be time to let our box of cheapos off. Sparklers would be the initiation to the screeches of the loud rockets and vicious bangers setting off and the more serene Catherine wheel and Fiery Jack being lit. Ever had a banger hit you on the chin? It bloody hurts I can tell yer... but then again, all those ads had been warning us non-stop for ages before the night, so what can you expect?

The night would end with a sad and desperate (slowly burning out) fire being scraped around to keep it going, no wood left for miles and all the taters and chestnuts long gone. If it hadn't rained already (and often it would have done especially for the occasion), then you could guarantee that it bloody well would now, just to lay a final dampener on things and put the final last few flames to rest... bastard weather, always ruins things. Oh well, it was now a case of looking forward to the morning after and collecting all the dead fireworks... Bonfire night was over and next up was Christmas.

When winter truly set in, then came the snow. The usual snowball fights would commence as soon as the snow was spotted after first looking out of the window. Nothing on this wide earth, back then, could drag kids out of their houses as quickly and excitedly as when it first snowed, and snow it did. Not the poncey wimpish shit we get nowadays, usually in the wrong month too. No... snow back then was proper snow. Nowadays the country comes to a standstill within hours, newspaper headlines spread widespread panic with stories that the roads are impassable, homes are blocked off and the supermarkets are running out of food. Back then, snow barely interrupted anything, except if the school boilers broke and we all had to go home and that was no trouble to us. Our parent's generation had survived a World war, so snowdrifts and ice was not gonna phase 'em either!

Cars would get covered in the stuff and we would watch fellas shovel the stuff away to reveal their dearly-loved cars: as soon as the bloke went in we would throw the snow back all over the car again. On one particular occasion, this bloke had seen us from his front window and he came out wanting to crucify us. He called us words that none of us had ever heard before, such was his anger at us, but we didn't care... it was just a laugh.

No harm meant. Besides, that bloke was an uptight mardy get and deserved a freshly snow-decorated car outside his house. We departed well amused.

Buses were a prime target for an avalanche of well-prepared snowballs. Our best attack spot was at the edge of the park near the traffic lights, where we would congregate around the old hut with a regimental sized line up of snowballs lying in wait for the next bus to come along. As soon as the bus appeared that was it... it was like those scenes from 'The World at War' with those rockets going up on the Russian Front. 'Zoom zoom zoom... Whack... whack... whack', almost all reaching their target. On one of these onslaughts the bus stopped and the driver leapt out of his driving seat straight out of the little window, leaving a bus full of passengers to look on as he furiously headed our way. Guess who he bleeding caught? Yours truly! What that understandably irate bus driver wasn't gonna do to me was nobody's business... he raged and raged at me holding me by the scruff of the neck. "He's gonna lamp me in a minute" I was thinking... but I think he thought the better of it. A 14 stone beast of a man beating the shit out of a ten year old kid might not have looked good. He calmed down a bit and scuffed me across the shoulder as if to say "next time boyo, next time." Even as he was stood giving me the works I had a bloody lovely Siberian-iced snowball in my hand behind my back. As he got to his bus, the temptation overwhelmed me... 'ZOOOOOOOM whack!!!' I wasn't usually that accurate with my throwing, but that one was a cracker! Straight on the back of the noggin' it landed... he must have been furious- poor lad! I was off before he could even turn around... thrapping like mad to get to the rest of the gang and tell 'em what had happened.

Another snowball victim included the Butler (a fella so named by Pete Roddis as the fella did look like a Butler, sideburns n' all). We were on our usual snowballing runs and we pelted every door and window on this particular street. Just as the Butler opened the door shaking his fist, a perfectly aimed jet-speeding snowball hit him smack bang in the chops!

The snow also provided us with the Battle of Oakwood Crescent v Warren Avenue one year. Following one really heavy snow season, with heaps of the stuff to play about with, one Sunday morning me and Andy decided to offer the whole of Oakwood Crescent out in a snowball scrap! Were we mad or just plain insane? Oakwood Crescent was home to a right likely bunch of lads and plenty of 'em too... they were rough, mostly big and meant business... and just cos one of 'em lobbed a snowball at us resulting in a bit of banter that Sunday morning, we had to go and offer 'em all out.

As the depth of our situation and challenge sunk in, we started to rally our snowball ammo together and accepting our fate of Kamikaze-styled demise by snow, we came to the conclusion that - like Davy Crockett at the Alamo - we may as well go down fighting. The word was on the street and the Crescent gang were congregating. A few lower ranks of our much-loved Warren Avenue were asked by us to join the cause, but they just laughed at us and went away shaking their heads at the thought of our request. Where's yer God-fearing neighbours when yer need 'em eh?

As it happens (to quote Jimmy Saville), we did manage to get some reinforcements to sign up. Our Glen and his new girlfriend, Lesley, saw our plight and impossible situation and decided to join in and help us... quickly gathering some much needed snowball ammunition together. As scouts were sent around the corner of Oakwood to see what our defences were, a new glow of confidence swept over us.

At this time, Andy was going through the uncomfortable time of having Tonsillitis and had merely popped up to mine for a bit of fresh air after being cooped up in bed for days. Wrapped up and ready to brave the elements, hoping to spend some quality mate time, Andy didn't realise the full extent of his visit out of Medical HQ, but even so, the lad was as brave as our two gobs were and we weren't gonna back down. As the drum rolls came closer and the crunching of jackboots hitting the snow sounded, we retreated back from our forward point down the street, back to our main defence line. "This is it" we thought ... "To hell or Victory." Zoom.... Some salvos sped overhead splattering on the wall beside us: here comes the first wave. Holding our fire, with our two older recruits in cover close by for the element of surprise, we bided our time to hit back. We could now see the forward troops from the Crescent regiment slowly making their way closer to our position... lobbing the odd snowball our way. Their first wave was now in range as their second wave appeared from around the corner. Glancing quickly across their force, we could see Bob Norton, Pete Roddis, Mick Lowry, the Hamilton brothers, the Souths (and the northerners too): a right motley gang of mercenaries heading our way, followed with the Clay clan pushing a barrowful of balls of pure ice behind them. My 'ead was throbbing with the thought of each impact making contact. "Let 'em have it" Andy shouts and our two conscripts stand up in view and whack a endless barrage of snowballs straight down the street knocking the Crescenters a bit off their feet and achieving our much-wanted surprise attack effect. We joined in and the barrage became more intense. A passing car, only managing to do a one mile an hour snails pace drive up the snow-laden road got pelted too; friendly fire does happen in war yer know!

By now, our enemy had received some stuffing knocked out of them as they stood their ground: shouts of "They've got their Glen and his bird with 'em— the sods" carried over to our line as we continued our relentless barrage of snowballs their way. But the barrage had to end sometime and we began to run out of snowballs, taking it in turns to replenish our ammo as quick as we could. There were some right full on face-felt impact hits going on and kids were starting to flag a bit, us too. But on came the enemy and on we had to fight!

The battle must have gone on a good twenty minutes or so by now: morale was still high on our side and ammo was being presented as quick as possible. Seeing the Crescenters start to flag and slip and slide about as missiles of ice hit and found their targets, we decided to make a charge at 'em. "Over the top fellas" was the rhetoric displayed as we gathered as many snowballs as we could and advanced swiftly down the field of battle towards our enemy... Ouch! whack!!!, yeouch' cries of pain went out on both sides... we were almost on them, but they were still throwing shells back at us: some of their smaller ranks fell by the way-side and got pelted with some shots to finish them off. As we inched forward and the air was full of rockets of snowballs zooming each way, laughs, cries and shouts of "Hold your ground"... Andy gets too close to their line and is captured!

The battle continues, but we struggle to hold our ground with one man missing: but then so do the opposing force as two of their ranks concentrate on dragging their prisoner away around the corner. As they do so, a couple of their Gestapo type party members rush over and dish out their torturous punishment on their prisoner. We watch helpless as they open his mouth and fill it full of lovely crisp fresh snow... hitting inflamed tonsil and sensitive tooth alike. The pain suffered by our comrade must have been immense: his battle was over. He crawled through the snow back to us as the battle died down and both sides retreated to their bases. Andy had paid the price, he was in agony. We patted him on the back for moral support. The two sides were now slinging insults instead of snowballs at each other... us saying they cheated by dishing out punishment contravening the Geneva convention and them saying that we cheated getting two grown ups on our side. The Battle of Oakwood v Warren ended that Sunday lunch-time with freezing hands, soaked feet, red faces, the odd bruises and a cauterised pair of Tonsils for poor old Andy. No one could agree on who won the battle, we all had our versions of events... but all would agree pain apart, that the struggle for street pride and total dominance and credibility had been one hell of a scrap and an even bigger one of a laugh!!!

....

Now, back then, like most houses, we would leave the back door unlocked at most times; certainly during the day. Neighbours would simply walk in, usually without knocking. The old saying goes that nobody had owt worth nicking so we were all safe from thieves and the like. That's not strictly true, especially as the 70's wore on. Our Glen now had a car, and that got vandalised/scratched with a pen-knife: him and our Paul put the feelers out and found out who it were and went round and sorted 'em out, a rough family around the corner. One of them was always grinning at me teeth gleaming just like chuffin' Burt Lancaster after a win on the Pools every time I saw him. He got right on my nerves that kid.
    Indoors we still didn't have that much worth nicking, so we often left the back door unlocked so me Dad could walk in after his night shift down the pit, or our Glen coming home from wherever he had been. One day, though, the next door neighbours' lad's motorbike got nicked and our Glen walked past the bloke who had got it without knowing. It ended up not just a thieving job, though, but arson too. It was about 1am and we were all asleep. Our Glen was due in and me Dad must have been either at work or it could have been when he had started to become more ill and was in hospital.
    Anyway around this time in the early hours, I was awoken by a smashing sound. I went into me Mother's bedroom to wake her up and when we

looked out of the back bedroom window, we saw a figure stood there looking into the next door neighbour's out-house. Shivers went down my spine as I saw that the out-house was actually ablaze. The bloke, all dressed in black, had smashed a fuel lantern deliberately to set it on fire. He had come to nick Stevie's bike, which he must have wheeled up the path onto the front ready to take with him; but not content with that, he decided to set the out-house alight as a leaving present. I was scared for sure. We got up and went downstairs just as our Glen was coming in. He had seen the fire as he came to our back door and we told him what we had seen. He then told us that he had just walked past a bloke in black wheeling a bike down the street. He went back out and the bloke was well gone by now, so he went and woke next door up and then went to the phone box on Walsh's hill (Kent Avenue) and rang the cops and fire services who arrived and put the fire out. We never did find out who it was who did this, the bike was found the next day all burnt out at the bottom of Kilnhurst road. My Mother swore that the bloke was a council worker that she had seen earlier that day working on our backs and had been taking an interest in the bike in the out-house. Can't prove owt, but it did make us all wonder.

Our street's criminals were few. There was the older lad (who gave us a push on our bogey) who lived across from us, and he was a bit of a bugger, to say the least; well he was always in trouble and had a right reputation. Me and my mate, Andy Goulty were once sat on me Mother's front wall and he came out swinging a coal poker at this bloke who was passing by who he had obviously got a grievance with. We thought it was hilarious, but the poor bloke thrapping down the street getting chased by this poker-wielding maniac certainly didn't. The assailant was always great with us, though. He even gave me some of his old annuals one day. He later went to prison and we were told by his Mum that he ended up in a cell with the Black Panther: apparently they used to play cards together!

The Black Panther (Donald Neilson) was a Bradford born multiple murderer and, for a while, was Britain's most wanted man. He shot dead a succession of sub-postmasters, battering to death another one before then kidnapping a 17 year old girl – Lesley Whittle. After a bungled ransom demand which led to Whittle's tragic death, he was apprehended by two policemen and consequently sentenced to life imprisonment in July 1976.

My Dad was coming home from work one day after his night shift at the pit and walked past a little fella with his head down wearing a flat cap. Turns out it was the Black Panther just after his Kilnhurst Post Office raid. Also, around this time, another extremely dangerous killer was gaining more and more notoriety and it became less safe for women to be out on their own. Sightings of the Yorkshire Ripper were common; he was even spotted at the bottom of our school gates... hysteria had started to set in a little bit.

Searching my family history has, so far, not revealed any murderers or kidnappers. Our family's only claim to notoriety was one of my Uncles who in the 70's was on the Dole and ended up cleaning the Dole office's windows when doing some work on the side. He did time in clink for that, would you believe! Really nice bloke too! Not exactly Hammer House of Horror then!

Our house did have its own Hammer Horror homage at the top of the stairs. On a cold, windy wet night with the addition of thunder and lightning completing the set piece - you could creep up our stairs and either run past the top of 'em and into your bedroom, or dare to peak at the window and the reflection of a bat's wing poking into the corner of the window. Our little Michelle was scared witless of this and if I mention it to this day, she gives a shudder... I used to drag my mates up to have a look at it and we were all intrigued at the sight. The scene right in front of us would have made a great scene in the opening credits of a Hammer Horror film! When we discovered that the bat's wing was in fact merely the shadow of a piece of guttering sticking out, the myth was dispelled, but for me, it was the bat's wing and still is!

I was now a full ten years old: bloomin' 'eck, it seemed like ages since I were a proper little kid. This was 1975 and I had loads of mates and we were having lots of fun. It was my last term of junior school so the train of thought amongst us all was to make the most of it, the fun will be over once we get to the big school. Me and Andy even performed a 'Jockey Gee special' on an older kid who was taking the mickey out of us as we passed. As the swine was grinning at us, we both looked at each other, read each of our minds and together, gave him a damned good push straight over his bush... followed by a good sprint off the road to these two sisters' house who were asking us to go round to see 'em later on. On thinking it over, curiosity got the better of us and we decided to go over the bushes and pay 'em a visit and were just about to set off, using their guiding in beacon of the Bay City Rollers singing 'Shang-a-Lang' ... when suddenly their Mother appears home... crap! I often wonder what we would have got up to had we reached our destination!

Speaking of the Rollers; in his typical eclectic taste (so rare for a ten year old) Andy went out and bought the latest Bay City Rollers LP, maybe in a juvenile wishful-thinking homage to fantasising what may have appertained had we made it past old Mother Ginger. I can honestly say I was not a Bay City Rollers fan at any stage. I suppose I already had enough dodgy musical likes without adding yet another one.

That year, 1975, though being the year of the 'Shang-a-lang' of the Bay City Rollers was also the year of 'Jaws' and it seemed that everyone went along to see it. I didn't! Don't ask me why not. I was interested, very interested, but it wasn't on the agenda for me that summer for some reason. I made up for it, though; by reading the original Peter Benchley novel and learnt lots of new filthy swear words I had never heard before from it. Good stuff to keep on record for the big school coming up. That year was also a kind of coming of age year for me in ways far more disturbing than watching people get eaten by sharks on a big screen. I had reached ten years old and had some growing up to do pretty soon.

1975 saw me take up drawing more seriously. I had always liked to draw and doing so with my school projects was probably the only thing I truly enjoyed at school at the time, apart from messing about, that is. The teacher wrote in my report of 1975 that my depictions of history and warfare have been a source of great pleasure to him. Nice to hear from a teacher that. It made a change from the usual "Tony has started to become extremely stupid" etc remarks. As I started drawing even more I even bought some proper artist's pencils. I also did do some paintings at school and some felt tip drawings, especially after watching our Glen do me a great depiction of a Planet of the Apes comic front cover. That really influenced me and encouraged me to try and do one as good as his.

I suppose most of my drawings would be classed as sketches, though. I would sketch scenes of warfare out of my annuals and books, front covers of my comics and some American Civil War illustrations I did for my school History project. One day, while my Mum was cat-napping drifting off from watching Googie Withers in 'Within these Walls', I decided to draw her. When I had done and showed her the depiction complete with every line in her face, she made me get rid of it and promise to never show it anyone... She was mortified at the sight and I don't blame her either! So drawing became a bit of a pastime, along with Airfix Models and everything else.

Some of my drawings from the time. I wasn't that obsessed with Planet of the Apes was I?

That year seemed to be the peak of my interest in Art. My mate Nicky Booth was a superb Artist, though, and I use the word Artist in a real way. He was truly amazing and one day, after seeing his exceptional work, I went home and threw away my proper artist's pencils, my interest in drawing in voluntary retirement for a while!

Around this time, I also left home too... Following a row with Mum and Dad I packed up a suitcase with all my comics and records and clothes in and set off out into the big wide world all on my own. I went up the path and left home for all of 15 minutes, coming back in, dragging the suitcase with me, and being met by faces indoors - busting to laugh at me.

By 1975, and increasingly, as the year turned into 76, my Dad's health - due to years of inhaling pit dust - had been deteriating progressively fast. His Hospital stays were getting longer each time and the air of seriousness on my Mum's face whenever the Doctor came to check on Dad was also getting more severe. I knew something was wrong, but no-one would fill me in with the complete truth. No matter what, though, despite his illness, my Dad still went out whenever he could. Sunday nights still saw him polishing his shoes to spick n' span army standard, him breathing ever shallower, and he would go up the path and stand at the gate contemplating the journey ahead up to the pub. No amount of my pleading for him to stay in and rest would stop him. By 7pm he was gone! It was almost a battle of wills between himself and his illness: he just would not give in; he would continue to live his life as much as he could. I don't know how much he knew of how serious his condition was, but it never got him down. He had incurable Emphysema thanks to the pit, but as long as he had an inch of breath left in him he was not going to give in.

I can remember asking the grown ups "Is my Dad going to be alright.'... 'Is he going to die?" And "What will happen to me if he does." ... "Will I get put into a home just like one of those you keep saying me, our Dave and Steve are going in if we don't behave." I was ten years old and was starting to feel something that I just couldn't quite figure out what it was. My world seemed somehow different. The fun was there still, the laughs, the mischief and the games were all going on, but inside there was something else going on in my decade-old mind. I was scared!

Years later, you find out all these things. You hear about all those psychological name-dropping words – anxiety being one of them. I did not understand it one bit though and I told no-one at all. My Mum had enough on her plate to start with and I had to act tough in front of my brothers and mates for sure. Besides what could I tell any of them anyway and my greatest fear, apart from Dad leaving me, was that I would be laughed at. I decided to try and ignore it all. It would go away. Dad would get better soon. He's in the hospital and on good pills so that should be enough.

A year or so prior to this – before he had started to get seriously ill, or at least to my knowledge at the time, anyway, I had had a row with my Dad, which were quite rare, as a) he was hardly ever in and b) when he was he was far too busy either sleeping off a boozing session or rowing with someone else. Whatever it was we were arguing about I really don't know now. Most likely I would have been arguing with Mother and she may have said "Tell him then Ken he's your son too", which he never seemed to understand the meaning of, his face saying "what the heck you on about" or I may have been rowing with our Glen cos he threw me across the room after lipping him or something! Anyway, whatever the reason, I lost my cool and went running into the pantry, grabbed a can of garden peas and threw them straight at my Dad, which landed full on at him at his chest: I didn't think they would hit him; I lost my temper and didn't care... I looked around and saw his face looking in despair at me, a look he had never ever thrown my way before. I think he was shocked more than anything. I felt remorseful, I withdrew and run out of the house, coming back later on to say sorry, But... he had already gone out and it was too late. I felt terrible!

My conscience was severely pricked, I deserved a damn good hiding and maybe I would have felt better for it, but it never came my way... the punishment would be far more far-reaching and profound and fitting the crime as its here to stay forever. I didn't understand why I reacted that way: I felt really low for doing that and suffered a lot in my head for it... infact I was truly ashamed and have regretted the act for the rest of my life! I had discovered that there was a side of me that I had not so far previously known, one that would reappear every now and again throughout my teenage years, and a little beyond. It was an inner rage and deep-rooted anger and it was a side of me that I really did not like!

Back to 1975, my Dad had had to be signed off at work around this time: even though his attendance was almost non-existent by now, his mates would actually do his work for him to keep his name on the books. But, it was no use, he was no longer a fit (or half fit) working man. He had not long since come into his fifties, but he had the lungs of a very old man, courtesy of a lifetime's worth of pit dust with no extractors as law had declared to be a legal requirement since around 1954. He would still go and see Grandma each and every Sunday morning and then struggle along to the Fighting Cocks for a few pints. He still struggled, but managed to get out on a Sunday night too, no matter how much we pleaded with him to stay in and look after his health. He would never listen, my dad, he did it his way every time. It was heartbreaking to see him get worse and worse, his breathing becoming more laboured by the day... and then he became bed-ridden. He had to retire to our front room with the bed being brought down, oxygen tank at his side and a whole host of varying shapes and sizes of tablets to be taken every day. I started to look after him while my Mother went out sometimes. I would be going up to the Comprehensive soon, so maybe it was time to start doing a bit of growing up.... And I wanted to show how sorry I was for being a rotten little swine and slinging that can of peas at him. We shared some happy times, laughing at things and people and watching Tarzan films together. It was tragic and one of life's strange turns: his illness had brought us closer together than ever!

The scorching summer of 1976! Who can forget that summer? We were getting hotter by the day and wondering when the sizzling melting heat was gonna let up. It was unreal: and none of us even looked at a tube of suncream, or knew of such a thing. Everyday we would go to school and be sweating like crazy. As we broke up from our last term at junior school, waving goodbye (or flagging two fingers) to our uptight teachers, well, the heat just got worse. Time to forget the prospect of the Comprehensive school in far-away September, summer was here, schools out and fun was ours for the taking! As we frazzled in the heat, time seemed to stand still for the whole six weeks holidays. The Junior school years had ended and now we were out there in a six weeks world of no mans land and digging the sounds of Chris Spedding's 'Motorbiking' while riding our Chopper bikes... we were neither junior school kids nor proper Comp kids.

That summer also saw the peak of what I would call novelty crisp snacks. I had been brought up on Golden Wonder crisps, ready salted (also known as plain), salt and vinegar and cheese and onion. No other exotic flavours or gimmick shapes, just plain old crisps. Other brands on the fringes were XL crisps, which always seemed to be broken up in bits for some reason, Murphy's crisp, Smiths (who had been the original crisp maker and were the only ones to do Bovril flavour... a lass on our street got nick-named by us 'Bovril face' after riding past us on a horse eating a bag of Bovril crisps). Also the light-weight classic school playground irreplaceable potato puffs, which were quite probably the messiest crisps you could get your gob round. Soon, though, there would be loads of new tempting novelty snack crisps in the shops. Bones (pickled onion flavour), the TV advertised Rancheros (like bacon nibbets on steroids with heaps of juicy flavour to them), Ringos, Quavers, Hula Hoops, Nibbets, Discos and the newly launched French Fries. Visits to the shops would see us returning with a bag of crisps in one hand and the other steering our bike all over the place. Back then bags of crisps had enough in them to offer your mates a handful as well... and it would be a bloomin' handful too, half of the time!

Around this time, I was enrolled upon to look after our Dave, Steve and Michelle while our Paul and Megan went out. As soon as they were around the corner, chaos would ensue as we got Mickey the dog over-excited and encouraged him to chase us all over the house, knocking ornaments all over the show and us sneakily gluing them back together again. Years later, Megan began to realise a pattern in far too many ornaments crumbling and breaking as she touched them, forcing us to own up. She never knew half!

The TV we watched on those nights was still saturated with American Cop shows including the newly 1975 syndicated Starsky and Hutch. This one was cool, though and full of action and car chases, and was essential viewing at 9.25pm right after Saturday Night at the Movies on BBC1. My heroes of the time, as well as Starsky and Hutch, were James Hunt, Kevin Keegan and even more so, Barry Sheene, who was the coolest sportsman ever to me. He had a cool girlfriend and an amazing Suzuki 500cc bike and just as importantly, for me, he stuck two fingers up to people from time to time. He had some real spirit. He recovered from a crash at the Daytona 200 in 1975 being broken to pieces and was fitted with enough metal body parts and pins to rival the Bionic Man (another hero of mine). I copied his race track moves on my chopper, going round corners with my knee scraping the floor and gradually shredding holes into my Falmers jeans. I adopted his bike number seven as my favourite number, placed stickers of him all over my bike and went out and bought those poster mags that were all over the place back then: a glossy magazine that folded out into a massive poster, ideal for my bedroom wall with my Planet of the Apes ones.

My musical tastes expanded a little when our Glen (when not journeying out to see local club Rock act Bitter Suite with our Paul) bought Queen's 'Sheer Heart Attack' on cassette for the car (as well as some more Bowie). Glen would impress upon me the merits of Brian May's guitar skills and we would listen to 'Flick of the Wrist' from the album. Via this influence I went out and bought 'A Night at the Opera' LP and became a short-term fan of Queen until 1977. Who can forget the video for 'Bohemian Rhapsody?' The rest of the music going in my ears was still the usual pop stuff and some bits of Disco that had gradually been taking over the music scene recently. Soon, that musical genre – and its accompanying epitome of 70's fashion gone wrong – would peak with the massive success of a film (very) loosely based on the club lifestyles of 1960's Mods, this time the story being transported to mid 70's New York... yes Saturday Night Fever!

Me and my mates had not yet started to take our fashion sense seriously either. Lumberjack shirts, dodgy Brutus jeans and those iron on sticky transfer type thing T-shirts with your name on that we had done in the Rotherham market. While trying my best to ride like Barry Sheene and shut out the thought of going up to the Comp in September, another hero of mine was slowly starting to lose his health. My Dad was getting worse yet again. His Hospital stays now stretching into weeks, if not more. Visits from the Doctor, when he was back home, seemed like almost every day. He was struggling to get up the stairs at all and the oxygen tanks were getting bigger and more serious along with countless new pills to take with the ones he was already on. I was starting to become very worried about him!

At the same time, I was entering a brand new phase of my life... physically too. As the excitement and anticipation coupled with a slight fear of the unknown set in... of thoughts of going up to the Comprehensive, I was also starting to see the first signs of puberty kicking in! Ummm, so this is what happens I remember thinking. Allsorts of strange notions of imaginative thoughts go through your head at that age and you really do wonder if it's only you who is experiencing it all. I can remember being laid on the settee watching 'Zulu' on the telly and suffering growing pains in my legs. I was stretched out and by the time Rorke's Drift had been declared safe again I had gained an inch and a half on each leg.... Or so it seemed! Also, suddenly, the thought of a peck on the cheek with a part-time girlfriend seemed not nearly enough and you start to take more notice of the lasses you know or see on the telly: Jaime Sommers suddenly became more enticing than simply for her Bionic strength: as for Susan George, well she was the biz! As my voiced started to slightly break and a sudden urge to cuddle and embrace and smother with French Kisses the opposite sex confirms something is going on below the waist that I had previously not known owt about... I realised that a lot of things I had been interested in less than a year ago, were now, no longer that cool!

Action comic No.1 (© Egmont UK Ltd)

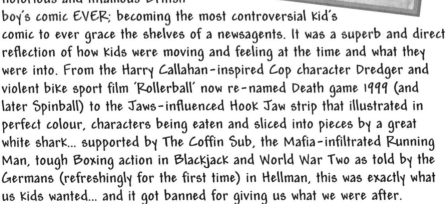

In-between worrying about (and trying my best to look after) my Dad (as best a kid can do), experiencing the first tickles of puberty, going out on my Chopper bike and knocking about with my mates, I was still up on comics. The trek to the newsagents was still firmly on the weeks' rota. As Valiant and Lion and some of the other stalwarts became boring a new comic came out around this time called Action!

Action comic was the most notorious and infamous British boy's comic EVER; becoming the most controversial kid's comic to ever grace the shelves of a newsagents. It was a superb and direct reflection of how kids were moving and feeling at the time and what they were into. From the Harry Callahan-inspired Cop character Dredger and violent bike sport film 'Rollerball' now re-named Death game 1999 (and later Spinball) to the Jaws-influenced Hook Jaw strip that illustrated in perfect colour, characters being eaten and sliced into pieces by a great white shark... supported by The Coffin Sub, the Mafia-infiltrated Running Man, tough Boxing action in Blackjack and World War Two as told by the Germans (refreshingly for the first time) in Hellman, this was exactly what us kids wanted... and it got banned for giving us what we were after.

The comic, which became known as the seven penny nightmare (my favourite number seven again!), was the subject of moralistic debates in Parliament, parents would try and stop their kids buying it from the Newsagents, its gore content was immense and it delivered the goods every week from 14th February 1976 to 16th October 1976 for its pre-ban run. A nation of soon to be young Punk Rocker kids became intoxicated with Action and its gritty angle to boy's comics and when it was banned in October it was a sign of things to come just around the corner.

Action comic arrived in perfect timing that year. Unfortunately, by the time of its post-ban re-emergence in December, from when it ran for a further 50 issues until November 1977, it had been diluted to a shadow of its former self and the blood-splattered colour of Hook Jaw had gone to black and white and almost all of its gritty no holds-barred appeal and gore had been lost. It remained a classy comic and I bought every single issue but it was never the same after the ban, eventually merging itself with Battle comic to become plain old Battle Action.

Also, around this time, I made the decision to take all of my Commando comics to Rotherham market's indoor book and comic stall and sell them all for a penny each. I had accumulated a great little collection of these, along with War Picture Library, Battle Picture Library and all of their summer specials and some Western ones too, buying them from either the spinning display stand at the Kiosk in Rotherham bus station at the side of the Omnibus café or second-hand from the comic stall itself. Now for a penny for each issue of these war-themed-action-packed picture strip pocket comics I let them all go and went along and bought Mud's greatest hits LP from the Sound of Music for something like £3.49... which means I must have had 349 comics to sell! From now on, comics were kids stuff: my regular orders began to be cancelled at the newsagents (apart from one I forgot to cancel – Tiger, which I was presented with a massive pile of to pay for after about a year or more... I kept out of the newsagents for a few weeks after that demand)... Comics had been and gone, loved and left behind and in its place was records and all associated with it. No matter, anyhow, Punk had arrived to replace the kid's comic strip violence with something more sinister and far more dangerous: the nation's public enemy's number one – the mischievous Sex Pistols had arrived!

Chapter Seven

I saw a Punk Kid the other day!

And the pit killed me dad!!

"September 76 and off to the Comprehensive we go. The anticipation had been one of worries about all the mythical scare-mongering stories we had heard of from other Kids (head down the toilet etc); but it was also a feeling of excitement and apprehension... though I didn't understand what those feelings meant... it was just butterflies in the stomach to me."

The red-hot blazing scorcher of a summer was still unrelenting when we saw the back of our last school holiday of the junior school years. It was the summer of masses of invading lady birds (we collected 100's of 'em and Kept 'em in matchboxes), water hose bans, lollypop mania, swimming baths every day to cool down and unknown to us - the first stirrings of Punk Rock down in the smoke!! For us long-haired wide-eyed lads it was the end of an era. We would be soon entering into a new world of bigger lads, tough 'uns who we knew nothing about. It was a time of change for many that September to Christmas 1976 period and pretty soon things would never be the same again.

My first introduction to secondary school life at Rawmarsh Comprehensive (or Haugh Road as we knew it) was an earlier visit from the juniors with our teacher. As I looked around me on our guided tour, I felt like I had entered into a world of KES!! The kids obviously were much bigger, the attitudes a lot more arrogant from the kids we passed, and the teachers also looked like extras from Ken Loach's classic film – one of them the exact double of the Head-teacher in the film. As we turned a corridor on B-Block, a teacher was wrestling with an older pupil: I am not sure, to this day, who was dragging who down the corridor – the teacher or the kid?? It felt like a different world altogether. All that was needed was the big-headed sports teacher and the scene would be set.

So, Tuesday morning... still the sun is shining and the heat is as unbearable as ever... this extended Indian summer still means serious business. The way we were going, we would be in short sleeves and shorts for Christmas. Holidays over; My mates Gary, Andy and Pete are at the back door. It's our first day at the big school and we are all bolstering each other up. *"Nowt to be bothered about lads"* was the Gung Ho! attitude as we walked the short distance to our new school, laughing and joking all the way to our five years of a new regime of education.

We get there and before you know it, we are all split up into different forms. New mates are made, kids from the other schools, kids I had never seen before... different names, different faces, all with the same interest, getting through our first day at the Comp!! New faces also meant new enemies too and it sometimes happens that as soon as you set your eyes on some kids you simply can't stand 'em. This was the case with a few kids I shared the same form with. We were never going to get on, no matter what.

Anyway, we survived the induction and by lunch-time, the butterflies have flown away, the inner fears have subsided and the nervous laughs are being replaced by questions of *'who does tha support'*, *"what music does tha like – 'Suzi Quatro or Mud... Rod Stewart and the Faces or David Bowie and Roxy Music...."* more importantly... *"Whose cock er thi school then"* and *"where is he?"* *"nowt to do with me all of that, let em sort it out* between themselves," I thought. Funny thing is, though, the big hitters very rarely got into a scrap and they hardly ever had a go at each other. It's the little gob-shites that think they are the tough 'uns that can't wait to set fights up and cause all the trouble. For the next five years, bar a few scuffles and black eyes and kicking a few kids about back, I kept out of that sort of trouble... saw plenty but stuck to my role... being a rebel with a joke! Soon the rebel in me would match up with a new music that would be tailor-fitted to my anti-authoritarian nature. I was born maybe two years too late to fully embrace this new music straight away and experience all the early sign-posts of the starting laps, but the attitude was already a part of me. I was already a Punk, but I just didn't know it yet!!

Quarter to four finish and sleeves are rolled up and we are off home. Thankfully we had also survived those quarter to four scraps when 100's of kids belted out of school looking like the cast of 'Spartacus'... all one thing in mind, wanting to watch the scrap at the bottom gates. Every time I saw that happen, I breathed a sigh of relief that it was not me going through that Gladiator-like fight initiation. The Romans had nowt on those lot!

6.30pm the same day and it's the very first school Disco of my life. Me and Andy Goulty went out and checked out the scene that night and managed to return to probably 95% of all the school youth club discos for the next four years. This first one was a bit of an eye-opener, I suppose. There were proper 14 and 15 year old lasses there and the music was proper Disco, Soul and hard as nails Heavy Rock. A certain faction of – out of time – kids were still crazy about 1950's and early 60's Rock n' Roll and would twist and jive away to Bill Haley's 'Rock around the Clock' and Chubby Checker, do the 'Woolly Bully' to Sam the Sham and the Pharaoh's and twist their ankles out of shape to 'Blue Suede Shoes' and 'Heartbreak Hotel.' As we were into Showaddy-bloody-waddy, we joined in with them, making complete prats of ourselves as the girls stood around watching us and justifiably laughing their heads off at us. It may have been out of time and scorned upon by the heavies, the Soulies and the Disco-ites, but this raw music sounded far fresher, more fun and vibrant than all of their cliquey musical spots. Even so, we were just kids, still, we didn't know what was really cool or not: we only came for the laugh anyway.

Looking around, at all of these varying sights and styles to view, all that denim, braces, fuzzy afro hair, long greasy hair, long leathers and flares abound, we, both, felt out of place but also at home. It was like we had entered into our own little Top of the Pops studio audience; a self-created world of all the fashion, music and things we had been reading about in the pop music mags and seeing on the telly pop shows. Tina Charles was telling us she loved to love and Pop heavenly utopia had arrived in our lives!

So this is what the bigger kids listen to and get up to then? These weekday discos were designed for each school year nightly or something, but a lot of people just went to whichever ones they fancied going to... After a while it settled down to your own years and younger, but us more adventurous kids would still go to the big un's discos, to which we were mostly made welcome... especially by the older lasses who thought we were cute and in their own Motherly ways, smothered us wide-eyed kids with breast-engulfing cuddles, bags of KP crisps, pop and sweets all to the sounds of Elton John and Kiki Dee singing 'Don't go breaking my heart', Showaddywaddy taking us 'Under the Moon of Love' and the Northern Soul of Derek and Ray's 'Interplay' and the feel-good vibes of 'Be Young Be Foolish Be Happy' by The Tams transporting us away from our school days. Not so bad after all, this big school lark is it?

As we had arrived at the Comp that first week, an older generation of kids were in their final year and a bunch of these, along with some who had already left, decided to go on strike. Me and my mates were on the way back to school after our dinner hour and saw a commotion kicking off. These lads were big 'uns and no one, not even the teachers messed around with them. A crowd of them, aided by a few girlfriends had marched out of school, met up with some of the year's school leavers and made their pitch right at the bottom gates. As we got there four or five of them had decided to lay down in the middle of the road, so the buses and cars couldn't pass. Others were shouting and cajoling passers-by and the approaching teachers on their way down the school drive. We thought this was hilarious. It took a while for the teachers to get them all moved and we ended up late going back into school, luckily our form teacher was late too. Probably due to the strike! Our first sight of open rebellion... cool!

It didn't take very long before I too was in trouble at the big school: I got the cane for snowballing the lasses when the winter of 76 saw a bout of much desired snow replace the almost year-long heat of summer. The head teacher knocked at our C3 studies class and beckoned me with his little finger. After a bit of a talking to in his office around the corner with me thinking that was it, he got his rotten cane out and told me to hold me hand out, which I did. Whack!!! My finger was visibly still vibrating as I went back into the class room with all eyes on me and whispers of "Beesley has just got the cane ha ha ha." A bit of playful antics with some snow and that's what yer get! Anyway, as much as I wanted to shed a tear, I bloody well didn't: the finger-whacking service only managed to service my resilience into not getting caught next time I do owt wrong. Trouble is, I did.

That next time wouldn't be that far off: I got slippered on a regular basis thereafter for giving teachers some lip. One time me and two of the lads even got slippered for falling asleep in Assembly. One of the totalitarians spotted us laid back doing ZZZZ's while the head teacher threw his boring sermons our way. Three of us he sent to sleep, it should have been him receiving the slipper for being so down-right bleedin' BORING!!!

Anyway, the little finger goes again and it was off to see old bos-eyed Mr Blackbeard after Assembly: this Mr Teach had a right twat of a slipper for a weapon, complete with a section of its leather bottom loosely hanging off, perfect to give yer a very sore backside and regretting falling asleep in dear old morning Assembly. The three of us took a right whacking and we made our way to our first lesson: one of the lads, a good mate of mine, was a right tough 'un that I used to knock about with and he had some serious tears in his eyes, poor lad, and made us promise to not tell any of the other kids. Like I say, he was a tough 'un, so we weren't gonna sprag, not that I ever spragged on anyone anyway, its one of my self-created ten commandments that- 'Thou shalt not sprag on thee mates, no matter what'. Not long after I got caught running around instead of going to a lesson. The rest of the class-dodgers got away and the teacher demanded their names from me, but I swore absolute loyalty and wouldn't give in, to which I got another slipper-induced leathering for my school kid morality. Another early slippering was dealt out to a whole bunch of us as we ran the Cross Country, following future local Athletics hero Peter Elliot but never keeping up. As we reached the second half of the scenic country run, flagging ramblers as we passed them, we took the short-cut straight across the farmer's field where the sports teacher, unknown to us, awaited with slipper in hand ready to whack us for cheating. Looking back, I don't think that there was hardly a single teacher that didn't end up giving me the slipper or cane... what did I do to them that got 'em so angry?

Those first few months of the Comp were exciting stuff, really. Everything was new and there was lots of stuff going on that we would never have been aware of back in the good old juniors. We would hang around with older kids and catch some of their swagger and attitude, that 'Don't give a sod' stance that comes with the secondary school experience... and it suited me no end filling in the gaps in my hidden inner rebel self.

These new teachers we had were different to the junior school ones we had had wrapped around our little fingers, one way or another. This bunch were mostly a clichéd throwback to the 1960's and smacked of that 60's intellectual idealism, I wasn't exactly sure of this at the time, but was aware of something linked to that decade, call it schoolboy intuition or something. My suspicions would be confirmed from time to time when these padded-shouldered sweater-wearing John Lennon worshippers and women's lib spouting exponents couldn't resist the obligatory Assembly sermon: one such preaching session being to the soundtrack of 'Hey Jude' by the Beatles. I mean, trying to convert kids that were supposedly the blank generation!

Talk about blank... there was our form teacher who seemed about as empathetic to us fledgling teenagers as Bill Grundy was to the Sex Pistols. From her confidence-building directions to A-Block, passing Mr Sweet Lips in a beard along the way, we would be met by a fruitcake Physics teacher (angry with himself for some reason) who had stepped straight out of a Will Hay movie. Steamed up double lens glasses, tweed jacket, greasy comb over top head, handle bars moustache and a truly eccentric nature to boot. His descriptions of what the laws of Physics meant to me was below zero, and consequently I learned physically zero. In the same old-fashioned post-WW2 trapped classroom, we also took Chemistry given to us by a lanky old Professor type with a gentle voice and a fog of self-interested obsession surrounding his rampant intoxication with his subject. How was I to get a look in, he had it all wrapped up in his own little world and didn't need any yawning bored-out of their heads kids interrupting his pastime.

There was one interesting thing about him, though. Supposedly he was there when the Hindenburg airship/Zeppelin burst into flames in May 1937. He saw it all and no kids believed him... I did! I also wondered if George C. Scott had seen him there?

Then came the two lessons that were totally new to us all. First woodwork, in which we were taught how to make useless household objects such as a spice rack (not even the spice we liked either): then came Metalwork and we were shown how to make a thimble!... A stupid bloody thimble, useful for one thing only, torturing other kids into parting with their spice or else get yer thumbs flattened... and that was the teacher dishing it out! Insanely, trusting us kids to be of a sensible and responsible mind, of which some swots certainly aspired to but I didn't, we were shown such dangerous activities as using lathes and machines that could maim and a white-hot furnace to heat up our metal so hot it could be re-shaped into something and then filed into further shape with a bastard file and some Dick Emery cloth. The greatest buzz ever in those Metalwork lessons was when we were all stood around watching and listening to Mr Bent-neck Balford displaying some casting tips and the like near the furnace. As we all watched a kid dip his rod into the heat until it was pure white-hot and then slowly turn around with it, I, and a couple of other lads could see another lad (another good pal of mine for a while) backing up towards the heated rod, oblivious to everything and his backside exactly parallel to the slowly travelling torture appliance. The urge to tell him was overwhelmed by the mischievous love of seeing what happens next and true to form and expectation the lad backed up his arse straight onto the white-hot thing. We were crying with laughter as the sizzle of bum meeting scorching hot branding stick grabbed everyone's attention. The teacher was livid; the kid was in a right state and had to have some cream applied to the frazzled area, poor lad. Never in the field of school kid v teacher relations has a backside been so burnt and frazzled and so many laughs given by so few.

Metalwork continued for a few more years and I eventually grew tired of it all, opting to either dodge the lesson and stay at home, forget my apron, or aim to cause some disruption and chaos to the class when boredom set in. But, I did design and cast a lamp shade to my own specifications, which took me over two years, so some skills were put to use.

Our Metalwork teacher was a bore. My new form teacher gave me a (well-deserved) good hiding for being more than a little impolite to him, I was sentenced to the back of the class permanently for Chemistry and our Sports teacher was chasing us for dodging lessons. Our Biology teacher, though, was something else. She was mature, a real woman and radiant with sexual chemistry that I couldn't quite figure out what it was all about, but my hormones were starting to send some previously unknown signals to me by this time and when she brushed past me with her large breasts and full-sized woman figure in a white smock, it sent a tingle through me. The lads were unanimously recognising these signals too and would circle Biology lessons on their time tables. Was Mrs Sex pot aware of all of this? I really don't know! I know one thing I was looking forward, excitedly to my next lesson when she had let us know it would be about reproduction... "woah, let's have some of this" we were laughing as we went into the classroom, our innocently over-imaginative sexual vision orientated minds in over-drive. Our faces must have dropped below desk level when she appeared from the dark depths of the back room with a bloody unborn small lamb, pickled in a jar, slippery, meths-smelling and eyes open. This was supposed to inform us of the fact that reproduction results in something else, in this case a bloody pitifully dead lamb that kept winking at me! Sexual hormones well in check lads eh! Mrs Sex Pot wasn't alone in attracting the drooling 12 year old pubescent lads to her inner teaching circle. One other teacher would openly talk permissively about sex to anyone who wished to listen. Proper sexual liberation stuff. A major draw her lessons were. We had arrived in September and by the start of the next year she was gone.

The new sex words we had learned- sperm, vagina, pubes, scrotum etc all were added to our swearing dictionaries, although in more vulgar terms, but at least we knew what the swear words all meant now. I was now a habitual swearer too, I had discovered lots of new and interesting words and found it fun to shout 'em out loud for anyone to hear. Out of school I wasn't too proud of my big gob when me Mother came around the corner one day hearing my expletives being broadcast. Oddly she never said a word to me, and carried on down to the shop. I would have been mortified if she had told me Dad! After a while the swear words lost a lot of their novelty and were left for future reference and possible ideal applications of use.

Teachers were often given a special limited edition treat of some choice ones now and again, though.

Me, Andy and the gang had finally started to look at our appearances too. No longer was it cool to hang around in t-shirts with your name iron-printed on with a picture of Evil Kneivel on. We went to Sexy Rexys in town and bought some proper flared jeans and also started to wear pin-striped trousers, cheese cloth shirts and wore cheap brogues with masses of segs in 'em, making us sound like an army on the march. Adidas t-shirts (when affordable) from Suggs Sports shop in town were also the coolest thing. We threw away our (until then) super cool skateboards too and off we would go wearing our new attire, hair swept back with sugar and water, to the youth club disco to listen to a musical diet of Disco Soul, plastic Soul, David Soul and Tina Charles Soul, hoping in our hearts, that we would manage to get a intimate smooch with one of the lasses from the year above that we fancied... and when it happened – and it was not that often – it was bliss!!!

Me and my mates, and occasionally our Dave in tow when he was allowed, were now paying a visit to Rotherham town centre on a regular basis, each and every Saturday afternoon, just about. We would call for each other early Saturday morning and catch the 107 bus to town. Getting on the bus, we would see the usual idiots, smoking fags and throwing stuff at people from the back of the bus. OK, we were idiots too, but not like these ones. We were after fun, and now we were starting to want to look cool. This lot were just trouble, full stop. Grinning their heads off at us and being maybe 4 to 5 years older, they would try and intimidate us, but we didn't care. The ring-leader had even tried shooting me and Andy one afternoon when we had gone on a trip down the woods. As we had seen him approaching us, we could see he had a rifle in his hand, possibly an air rifle? He grinned, lifted it up and took aim at us. We took a quick dive into the bushes as the whiz of shots missed us by inches. Years later, I think, just about everyone of that lot ended up in clink at some point or another, one (the Woods sniper) going down for a hefty sentence for a very serious crime many years later!

The bus journey to town was so much different then to how it is now. Progress has got rid of much of the local character we were so used to and had great fondness for. The massive iconic Parkgate Cooling towers are long gone, the Steelworks, pubs, railway junction all replaced by a more modern day set of business and consumer enticing developments. We even had a Woolworths and a proper record shop in Parkgate!

Town too was a totally different kettle of fish. You couldn't walk for bumping into people and everywhere you looked there was real shops. Wilson Pecks, Muntus, Brooks' café with its constantly addictive coffee aroma, Wigfalls (where my Mum had a constantly running debt for household goods and would queue each week after Dad's pay day to pay), Cantors furniture store (where mum also had a never-ending debt that she would pay each week), Timpson's shoes, Rumbelows, March the Taylor 'suits you well' (where Dad had a debt, but Mum had to pay it), C & A, Sexy Rexys' (we never got to meet Rexy though), Jefferson's photo shop (who also sold cassette albums on a spinner) and lots of other proper shops and

Assistant Margaret sorting stock in the Sound of Music Record shop

stores. Our younger days of visiting Topps (upstairs for the toy dept) and Coopers Toy shop and the indoor market comic stall was now replaced by excitable visits to the iconic 'Sound of Music' record shop and all the other record-selling outlets: Circles, Britain's upstairs, Woolworths and the second-hand stall on the outside market that only sold ex-juke box 45's.

The Sound of Music record shop had opened around 1969 and was a family-run business. Daughter Margaret put in the hours and commitment and if they didn't have a particular record you asked for, they would get it for you! The shop still had listening booths situated in there. The records in the charts were behind the counter, so you asked for them. Soon, we would delve much deeper into the real interesting music that was on offer in the shop, but for now I was satisfied with the usual chart crap!

Rotherham Statis fair 1970's

As well as the record shop visits, we were also stretching our independence to venturing to other places. Me and Andy went fishing at Greasbrough dam taking care to avoid the bloke going round the dam checking for fishing permits... of which we did not have. When the fun-fair came to town we went there too. The fair was near where Tescos and the police station now stand and was a huge affair, or so it seemed to us young oiks. A little gang of us would go in the evening and mainly hang around and soak it all up, watching the Waltzer and Speedway and taking care to not bump into any of the bigger kids hanging around that would probably give us a thump with no hesitation. A scary tall fella in a greasy filth-laden overcoat and a strange flat cap that we swore was actually sewn to his head, would be there chasing everyone around. His insane face scared me like hell, with his tongue permanently protruding and eyes rolled back, he stank of oil and in later years we nick-named him Big Mensi.

There was a sense of danger at the fair, something you can't really explain exactly, but it was there as the night drew in and darkness slowly came accompanied by all those sights, smells and sounds. It was something that kind of scared me, but also enthralled me. It was a danger not unlike the attraction to Punk Rock that would soon be engulfing me!

I can recall the exact day that I first truly thought about Punk Rock in any notable sense. The reason I can remember is that it was New Years day 1977 and I was laid on the settee in my Mum's living room... I would often lay there, sometimes with growing pains, but mostly just contemplating stuff: what I was gonna do next etc. That day, for some strange reason, I was thinking about Punk Rock! At that point, I really didn't have a clue what it was all about. I had seen the headlines, heard the teachers cursing the thought of these dirty foul-mouthed Punk Rockers and knew that there was a band, who were some kind of leaders of it all, called the Sex Pistols. I had seen them mentioned in a music paper I had bought from the shops for the charts. That January tea-time, I had a hour or so just doing nothing and for some reason Punk Rock filled up my blank thoughts! I wondered what it was all about, but I really did not have a clue. Why is it winding people up so much? If it's so rebellious and mischievous then, quite possibly, there may be something in it for me? Or maybe not? Time would tell?

....

January 1977: What was going on? I was collecting Green Shield stamps and hoping to get something from Sheffield with em when we went up in our Glen's car that Saturday. If I used the stamps, or if Mother or our Glen did, I am not sure... I opted for a trip into Redgates toy shop off the Moor for some more Scalextric track (or was it a Hump back bridge?) and an Airfix tank. Scalextric was going through a bit of a revival for me and my mates around this time, for some reason. Maybe it was a last grasp at staying young following our initiation into the world of the *big school.* Whatever, we had got the bug again and were extending our versions of Brands Hatch and other circuits we could copy out of the Scalextric catalogue. This era was also a time of the last bouts of interest in 'The Six Million Dollar Man', 'Happy Days' on a Friday before the youth club and the Saturday morning ritual of the Multi coloured swap shop: why did we watch with so much mouth-watering interest at what kids from the other side of the country were swapping their knackered old Action man for... why did we always think that one week someone on there would want something that we had... and even if they did, would we have really made any effort to join in with the whole swapping shebang? Would we heckers like!

February 77 saw another bout for my Dad in the old hospital on Moorgate. Sadly I had long since gotten used to all of this and it had become kind of normal for me to be visiting my Dad in Hospital once or twice a week. I remember the Doctor taking my Mum aside for some serious words around this time. I knew it wasn't good, I could see it on her face when the Doctor had gone. She never let on, though, and never told me until years later, that the Doctor had told her that my dad had maybe a year left to live. His Emphysema was getting much worse, his Oxygen intake and pills could only help out for a limited time now, she was told. I don't think my Dad was told... the Medical profession had some bleeding sense back then and didn't necessarily feel the urge to tell a dying man (or woman) how long they had left to live. How can you measure a man's life anyhow? I wasn't told what was wrong, but I weren't daft, well I was, but I did know all was not well. I decided to up my care for my Dad even more after that day.

Easter came and me and my Dad watched the biblical epic 'The Greatest Story Ever Told' awaiting the appearance of its so-called star, John Wayne. When he came on screen right at the end with his immortal one liner "Well surely that was a man of God" or something similar in typical John Wayne yankee drawl... well we took one look at each other in disbelief, then both burst out laughing... "Go 'n put the kettle on Tone." Dad laughed!

'Summer 77 came and the Queen's Jubilee was all the news (along with the naughty Sex Pistols and their apparent sabotage of it all) a new library in Rotherham opened and another new comic appeared - 2000AD. I bought it for about six months or more, but never warmed to that one; comics were now almost a bore! Around this time, June 1977, I managed to get my first proper serious girlfriend, well as serious as you can get at our ages. It was at the youthy, where else, that we got hitched up together. I had been sat watching the lasses dancing to the Disco and Soul on offer, me looking sullen and bored - a perfect clichéd expression for the summer of 1977 - and before you knew it, we were staring at each other in the Park after the Disco was over and decided on a good proper long kiss! I went home that night jubilant and feeling euphoric. My new girlfriend, Denise, was probably thinking "What a plonker!"

For a few weeks, that summer of 77, there was me, Denise, her mate June and her boyfriend Robo and we all hung out together without a care in the world. We biked to their houses, went to their Jubilee party to scenes of hilarity at the sight of two Mothers in scarfs and rollers whacking each other with sweeping brushes and two lads squaring up to each other with fists held high at Queensbury rules design. We went to parent-free houses for snogging sessions to a soundtrack of the Real thing, Hot Chocolate and Boney M and we dragged our bikes all the way down one side of the Roman Banks, across the busy road and all the way up the opposite side of the Roman Banks for another snogging session with our girlfriends. It was a great time and I didn't have a worry in the world. A few weeks later, all of us parted, except Denise and June. Well, they were lasses, they stuck together and they did also live next door to each other! Oh well, back to the bike-riding!

That summer saw me and my mates go through a fad of going around terrorising our neighbourhood on our bikes and dispensing of our bags of crab apples wrapped on our handle bars at peoples windows. We sped all over aiming as many as we could at families sat watching the telly in their front rooms, blokes mowing their lawns and O.A.P's innocently washing the pots. One such O.AP's window smashed on impact from our precision bombing attack. The next day the police came knocking at my door. I was at the table having my dinner and my Mum answered the door and I peeped around the corner to see her poor face drain of all colour. She would stand for owt, trouble-wise, my Mum, We were only kids and mischievous young soon-to-be teenage lads too, so she gave me plenty of lee-way with bovver, often telling the angry parent at the door to bugger off, and then giving me a telling off once they had gone. But the police? No she couldn't take that. "You ever bring the police to this door, Tony, and I will disown you" was her regular proclamation. Well, this day I did, but luckily she didn't disown me. The cops gave me a good telling off and said that I would have to pay for the damage, along with the rest of the gang. As soon as the boys in blue had scarpered, I zoomed straight down to my accomplice in crime,

Andy and unsurprisingly they had paid him a visit as well. Did we cough up the cash to pay for the broken window? Did we 'eck! One more lucky scrape we got out of in the end.

As the summer got hotter, so did people's ideas and actions. Our mate Gary fancied the hell out of an older lass up the street and would never stop talking about her. His stirrings were anything but the usual "Cor, I could snog her" stuff. He had designs on her... but, unfortunately, he never got anywhere with her. An older kid who was great at that kind of stuff called Bob Norton beat him to it.

This lass was from a new family on the block and I went out with the younger sister, who was about the same age as us. Her Mum and Dad were volatile so our short courtship was never disclosed to them. One evening, that summer of 77, as the sounds of Brotherhood of Man's 'Angelo', 'Sir Duke' by Stevie Wonder and the Sex Pistols 'Pretty Vacant' were blaring out of the radio some kid always had with the gang, we all congregated around the front of their house, just hanging around to begin with. When the parents went out to the boozer, we all jumped over the wall and paid a visit to their back garden. My awkward snogs with my girlfriend took second place, when some of the lads in the street gang started throwing stones and then bricks over in the direction of their back garden shed. Soon stones turned to fist-sized bricks and more and more kids joined in. Before long the scene looked like the Battle of Crecy with projectiles flying endlessly at the shed, smashing the window to smithereens. Once the initial damage was done, no-one held back and it was a free for all. I couldn't tell you why we suddenly turned to this act of wanton vandalism without a shred of conscience or care about the consequences. We all joined in, it was fun and almost euphoric... ok it was a buzz!

We were all laughing; the glass was all over the place and the lasses were not one bit bothered, some of them even joined in. The next minute we heard a car pull up. It was them, the parents, calling back early after they had been rowing. As they fell out of the car, they were still shouting at each other and we all heard them. I had never seen so many kids scatter in all directions ever before as that moment. We were all over the place, leap-frogging garden bushes, some falling down and not making it. Within seconds all that was left - we could see as we peered through from a nearby hiding place in a garden across from their place - was a shattered, window-less garden shed and stones and bricks spread all over the grass. The parents didn't even flinch. They continued their heated argument with each other as we all re-gathered on the street. The hilarious incident concluded with them both coming outside with a wall ornamental brass sword apiece fencing with each other in the street as we watched on. Can being young get any better than this, we thought?

Of course, when you are having fun, there has to be a soundtrack and the time was fast approaching for a small section of us to require something more exciting than the usual mainstream pop stuff we had been listening to. We needed to add some extra ingredients to our record buying and what better place to explore was there than the Sound of Music in town. In the shop they had masses of stock filed in racks and the singles in picture sleeves, including the handful of Punk records that had so far been released, were in PVC sleeves and then stuck to 12" sized card, all filed alphabetically for browsing through. As well as catching a glimpse at the likes of the rows of Rod Stewart, Roxy Music and Black Sabbath albums, I saw the first Clash album amongst the tiny handful of albums bunched together under a heading of New Wave. Its friends were 'Rattus Norvegicus' by the Stranglers, Television's 'Marquee Moon', Ultravox and 'My Aim is True' by a bespectacled fella called Elvis Costello! I would stand and stare at that Clash album, not really knowing what it represented and absolutely no idea what it may sound like. It would not be that long before that record would be a massive influence on me and become a lifelong vinyl friend!

The youth club disco was still the place to be for me and my mates. We would go three or four times a week. There was still lots of Northern Soul fans on the go (a type of music I had no real idea about, thinking it was linked to David Soul, but one which would enter my musical CV some years later) and plenty of long-hair, flares and denim. Heavy Rock came second to Northern Soul at the Disco and behind them were a couple of hour's worth of trash such as Paul Nicholas, the infernal 'Isn't She Lovely' and the safe and sweet sounds of good old Abba. There was no Punk Rock round our way yet, not that we had seen or heard of so far anyway.

One July early evening on a Saturday, I was heading up to see our Dave and Steve on my Chopper for a lark around. I got to almost the bottom of

Jackson Crescent and saw a bunch of kids crowded around someone... I could just make out our Dave amongst the gathering. Curious, I slipped into first gear and sped onwards to the meeting. Bike pulled up, brakes slammed hard and back wheel spinning, I arrived at the small crowd of kids and their encircled novice of a lad. What was so interesting and intriguing enough to stop the kids playing footie or 45 on a Saturday night, the best night of the week? This must be good? I jumped off my bike and caught the reason why. It was a real live Punk Rocker!

There he was, bleached (almost white) blonde hair in spiky fashion... looking like a new wave version of Joe Brown. Zip-covered red trousers... yes red... tight straight-legged yes straight not flared!!! leopard skin tight T-Shirt and badges that said words like 'Clash', 'Adverts', and 'the Damned' three times. This was amazing! This Punk Rocker wasn't swearing and spitting at us though, he was laughing and joking and answering the many stupid questions he was being bombarded with from us kids. "Where you going then, dressed like that... you can't be thinking of getting on the bus like that surely" were some of the comments. Back then getting on the bus was a big thing, it broadcast to all on there who you were, what you were wearing, what gang you hung out with and where you were heading... The Punk Rocker was off somewhere to see some Punk Rock band. He looked like nothing I had ever seen before in my life.

The opposition was cheese cloth shirts, Leo Sayer-styled dungarees, bell bottom flares, collar length and beyond hair styles and platform shoes, and they were the young generation! The Punk and his display of Day-Glo colour and air of disorganised fashion; the 'couldn't care less' attitude and image of rebellion had a direct and profound effect on me. Maybe I could look like that? I certainly wouldn't be able to go to those far away Punk Rock places and my Mum and Dad would never allow me to have my hair cut like that, never-mind the colour... but maybe there is something in this Punk thing that is right up my street. The Punk Rocker's name was Bryan; "Call me Bry lads" he laughed as he parted our inquisitive gathering and onto the 107 bus. We were left dumbfounded and I was amazed and captivated. Bryan Bell was the first Punk Rocker I saw: I would later become mates with him too. For me this, my first real meeting with Punk, would be the end of the seventies as I knew it!

The great six weeks holiday was here! As we anticipated if Geoff Boycott would hit his 100th century at Cricket and tried to re-enact our version of the Test Match, the summer reached its peak of headline-grabbing outrage with Punk. The nation had reached its highest level of intolerance towards these so-called nasty Punk Rockers. Reading the music weeklies each week saw some new account of anti-Punk activity. In our Northern pit town, being a Punk Rocker was even more of a statement. One such local early Punk Rocker who was also a friend of Bryan Bell was Russell Brookes.

Russell was the very first Punk Rocker amongst a small bunch of like-minded local music fans. Although openly a quiet and very likable lad, the arrival of Punk was an instant waking up call in his life. He immediately embraced the D.I.Y appeal of Punk, enlisting his Mum and sister to cut his hair as 'rough as they could', almost making his Mum cry. Such was the effect that early provincial Punks had: curtains twitched and fingers pointed at Russell and his mate - in their home-made Punk attire - as they set off down the street to go and see their favourite Punk bands. Russell soaked up all of Punk's initial sounds and styles and ideals; from the Sex Pistols, The Clash, Slaughter and the Dogs and everyone in-between, but his greatest Punk passion was for The Jam. He identified most with Weller and remained loyal to The Jam right through to the end! Sadly Russell passed away a young man, whilst in his sleep, due to complications with his health. At his funeral the sounds of The Jam's 'Down in the tube Station at Midnight' were played!

At the time Bryan and Russell (above) were almost exactly four years older than me. I would have to look lively if I was going to catch up with these proper Punk Rockers! In Rotherham, we suddenly noticed that there were Punks around. I would see some of them hanging around the old Ring o' Bells café at the bus station, I also saw them being chased off by some

brutes that look a bit like my favourite band Showaddywaddy... Teddy Boys!
I also saw some spiky-haired coloured-haired Punks in the Sound of
Music Record shop buying records I had never heard of, after listening to
them in the sound booths in the corner of the shop. I saw Bryan Bell once
or twice around this time and said Hello, but that's all. He seems to know
these other kids with coloured hair and ill-fitting torn clothes and hair
shaped like half-cut bushes and bog brushes. One day, that late summer,
while returning from visiting my Dad in the Hospital, I see a small gang of
these kids, even a couple of girls amongst their midst dressed in their
versions of this new fashion, all of them heading out of town toward the old
fair ground and then continuing onwards towards the football ground. What
could they be going there for on a Thursday night?

August 77 and I had my long shoulder-length hair cut round at the hair
dressers round Thorogate. "Why do you want your hair cutting short Tony"
asks the hair dresser. "Its more fashionable to have it longer" she
continued. I don't answer... I am not entirely sure myself to be honest. I go
to the Youthie with my new hair cut, which I have now attempted to sweep
back looking more like a 1920's gangster than anything remotely
fashionable. I have a pair of pin-striped trousers on, white tennis shoes
and my Denim jacket. The shirt I wear underneath is a red Adidas tight
fitting one. The kids in the Queue are all looking at me wondering what it is
I am into. I don't know myself so I can't tell them.
    Meeting the usual gang we all play table tennis, table football and listen
to the music on play in the hall. 'So you win again', 'The Crunch' by the
Rah band, Space 'Magic Fly', Jean Michelle Jarre's 'Oxygene part one' the
intoxicating hormone-awakening electro disco of 'I Feel Love' by Donna
Summer and then as we head into the hall and up the steps to the pop and
crisp counter a ridiculously fast drum roll kicks in after 'Angelo' by the
Brotherhood of Man... 'It gets my attention. What's this?' A screaming
barely intelligible voice kicks in followed by a chorus of 'I Don't wanna be
like You'. Its 'Looking after Number One' by a new Irish band called the
Boomtown Rats. The first Punk Rock record that I really like. 'Peaches' by
the Stranglers was ok earlier that summer, but till I heard the follow up
'Something Better Change', also around this time, I didn't even realise the

connection to Punk! 'Do Anything You Wanna Do' by Eddie and the Hot Rods soon follows, The Adverts on Top of the Pops with 'Gary Gilmore's Eyes' and then its time for the Marc Bolan show and my initiation to a life-long love affair with The Jam via their performance of their new single 'All Around the world'. This is more like it. These guys really look cool. I rip out the centre page Jam poster out of that week's Look in comic and back my C3 Studies jotter with it. A Lass called Tracy, who I never would have figured to be at all up on Punk said that The Jam are cool on spotting my Jam-hugging school book during the next lesson. I am impressed!

As she was admiring my new wave-adorned jotter, a whoosh through the air was heard and as I looked up a blackboard rubber hit me right on the chin. Now, I can tell you now. I had had the slipper off almost every teacher I had come across, from the juniors onwards and I had received a good whack from the head teacher with his cane twice. I had been given far too many good clips around the ear-hole that I care to remember, but I can tell you now, that bleedin' black-board rubber on the chin, at that speed, was the King of them all!!! It absolutely ripped! The pain on my jaw was bloody horrible and my bottom teeth felt like rubber. The teacher that day had suddenly become the perfect marksman and I had been the perfect victim!

My best mate Andy Goulty had also tuned into this new look at pop music almost at the exact time. He bought the Stranglers single in picture sleeve; suggests that we try a visit to Sweeny Todd's hairdressers on Bridge gate in Rotherham town centre and see if they can do us our hair like these Jam fellas. We go on a Saturday morning, nervous as hell watching all the fashion lovers getting their hair done like footballers and Rod Stewart. Three quid they want off us to have our hair done... three blinkin' quid? Our whole week's spending money in one go, bar our 2p bus fare home. That hurt almost as much as the black-board rubber on the chin that did. Three quarters of an hour or so later we come out with our new hair styles. Soft fly-away fluffy-spikes with headphones over our ears, we head off to the bus station and home... not really daring to peek at ourselves in shop windows. We both eye up the other though, and not one of us laughs... and believe me, we would have done if the slightest chance of a piss-taking jibe was at hand. So we must have looked at least a bit cool.

When we get home we start making lists of all the records that we wanted to buy. Within weeks the lists were formulating. Autumn was here, Elvis Presley had died on a rainy Thursday and a horrible record saying it remembered him was in the charts. For us, though, new sounds were emerging and becoming more and more enticing. Andy noticed lots of colour photos of Punk bands in his 'Supersonic' magazine: we learn a lot about the new bands in there and the weeks old NME'S and Sounds we bought loads of in banded together batches from the newsagents on Bridge gate. Andy then bought 'The Modern World' by The Jam from Circles record shop after that Thursday's Top of the Pops appearance. Then it was '2468 Motorway' by the Tom Robinson Band, 'Black Betty' by Ram Jam band (not Punk at all, but we didn't know), Stranglers 'No More Heroes', 'Mary of the Fourth Form' by Boomtown Rats and before the year was out Andy had got two serious Punk LP's 'New Boots and Panties' by Ian Dury and the Blockheads and 'Never Mind the Bollocks' by that band of misfits the Sex Pistols. The road to being a part of the Punk generation was almost at an end... we were banging on the doors to be let in, we had very little idea what it was all about, we didn't even take it that seriously... but there was something that we really liked. We may have still been wide-eyed clueless kids but we were in for the ride, Punk Rock was for us and we wanted a part of it!!!

By this time, almost all of my interest was focussed on music and all of its associated paraphernalia; from the records, Top Forty run-down on Sundays, magazines, patches, badges, pop logo-mirrors and scrapbooks. It was a full-time pastime just about and the age of discovery was upon us. We knew what number a record was in the charts and what number it was last week and the week before, we were that obsessed by teen-pop culture. Sadly an icon of my very earliest pop star likes - via my brother's records - Marc Bolan, was taken from us at a far too young age that September. I continued to play what were now my Marc Bolan records and never stopped digging the sounds of old T-Rex!

Aside from music and the camaraderie of hanging with my mates, I was also still up on films. This being years before the advent of video renting and recording, we still depended upon the telly for films and the occasional trip to the pics. In 1976-1977 I saw, amongst others, 'Futureworld', 'The Gum-

-ball Rally', 'The Battle of Midway', 'Airport 77' and 'A Bridge Too Far' at
the cinema, the latter re-enforcing the fading obsession of Military
History that was unfortunately taking a poor second place in my interests,
along with the runner-up of my Formula 1 and Motorbikes fascination. By
now, music spoke to me like none of these no longer did and was much
more fun and exciting!

Christmas 1977 was on the horizon: Star Wars reigned supreme in the
cinema - though I never warmed to the phenomenon. Muppet fever sweeps
the country, Wing's 'Mull of Kintyre' remained forever at no.1 in the charts
and our Glen bought a puppy while my Dad was in Hospital. The cutest
puppy I had ever seen and I just wanted to stroke her till next week and
back again. My Mum says "Wait while yer Dad comes out of Hospital, he will
go mad at yer Glen, he won't have a dog in the house you know that." I
think the last dog we had was an over-excitable one that never stopped
running around the house and would only stop to give me a nip on the arm
as it passed, the little git! That would be about 1969 or thereabouts and it
soon was got shut of. I named this new dog 'Sheena' after the Ramones
song 'Sheena is a Punk Rocker' I heard on the radio; quite appropriately
named as it turns out, when Sheena starts to get into her stride and wrecks
the house and eats and chews her way through everything each time she is
left alone in the house. She certainly created some anarchy that's for sure! I
never did get to embrace the Ramones for sometime, though Andy did, but
I knew I had chosen the right name for Sheena- the Punk Rocker. Next we
need a Punk Rock cat!

So what did Dad make of the worlds first Anarchist Punk dog? He came
out of Hospital for Christmas, only just though as he was very nearly kept
in: he took to Sheena straight away, made no fuss at all and was best
friends from the start. What was all the fuss about?

Christmas Eve 77 saw me and Andy (our nick-names were now Buzz
and Gola respectively as chosen by our good mate Shaun Angell) guitar
miming to that old over-roasted chestnut 45 'Merry Xmas Everybody' by
Slade in my Mum's front room (a kind of tradition for me and Andy); The
Goodies Punk special was still being applauded by myself and Andy and we
were looking forward to 1978 with great excitement. We now officially
proclaimed that our favourite music was not Rock n' Roll, Disco, Glam

Rock, Heavy Rock (or the hard stuff as we termed it) but Punk Rock. It may have been over down south and for the originators, but we were only just starting so don't tell us we can't have a piece of the action!

Back to school is so depressing after Christmas (and following the six weeks holidays and Easter and Whitsuntide and every weekend for that matter). January 1978 and me and Andy were really kicking into gear with the New Wave. He shot straight into the Buzzcocks and the Patti Smith Group, I went crazy on The Jam ('Modern World' LP too, 75p from Britain's Dept store's New Year sale) and The Clash and the both of us were enthralled by the Stranglers, Elvis Costello and the Attractions and the Boomtown Rats. Other  records of interest came along... X-Ray Spex, Radio Stars, Rich Kids, Squeeze, the Joan Jett led Runaways, Generation X, Tonight etc. Top of the Pops now had at least two New Wavers on each week and I would listen to the dismissive comments from our Glen saying "Look at these idiots', summat up with 'em" etc. He didn't know that his little brother was now a fledgling Punk kid. Maybe he might have noticed a change in my look (me and Andy must have looked more like Victorian street urchins than typical Punks, though) and an attraction to these short-haired yobs now infiltrating Thursday night's Top of the Pops, but he was none the wiser to my new musical heroes of the day.... Or so I believed.

One day, roughly around this time, after catching me getting over-excited at The Jam performing 'News of the World' and Elvis Costello's 'I don't want to go to Chelsea' on the Pops, he says to me "C'mon then, let's have a look at all these Punk records tha's been hiding away in the front room cabinet." "Shit my cover is blown" I was thinking... so I goes and gets my pile of singles and two LP's from under the Abba, Boney M, 10cc and Queen collection. A quick inspection of these unusual looking records (mostly in pic sleeves) and a muttering of "That's not Punk" at a couple of em and it's a comment of "What a load of rubbish, why yer wasting yer spending money on that lot, get some proper music bought." But, musical tastes aside; he had the good heart to buy me the Boomtown Rats 'Tonic for the Troops' LP for my birthday. Unfortunately, when he gave it to me, I already had been out and bought it! My enthusiasm was so keen by now.

Back at the very start of the year, I had a boil on the cheek of my arse and could hardly move for a week. I was worried sick about my Dad, who was getting worse with his breathing and illness. He was starting to get delirious at times too and talking daft stuff. He was getting out of his downstairs bed in the front room less and less now and was looking very ill. I was getting very very worried. I think that worry gave me that boil on me arse. That's my theory for what its worth anyway.

Rewind a bit more slightly and just after Christmas, through some weird type of extra sensory perception... I was having some really worrying (what we would now term) anxieties. I was starting to get a regular nagging feeling that my Dad was going to die soon. It was on my mind every single day and it was starting to become a major worry for me. I had this overwhelming persisting kind of inner voice that was telling me that he would not be around for much longer. I remember that I began to consciously make sure that I did as much for him as possible. I spent many hours just being near him, while he either chatted to me, smiling and laughing at my poor jokes and stuff about school or I just stayed around while he slept, waiting for him to wake up and ask me what time it was or ask me to get him something.

Looking back it became a very lonely world for me those few weeks of early 1978: my only respite was going down to Andy's to play our new Punk records. I couldn't tell anyone how I felt. I wasn't brought up to show my emotions anyway or to admit that I had any kind of a worry. You just acted tough no matter what: crying, feelings and being worried about things were a sign of weakness and it was a case of you just got on with things. It wasn't a bad way to grow up and had done me no harm so far. The trouble is, no matter how much I got on with things, I couldn't shake off this endless worry and sense of something was going to happen to him. I tried to hold on mentally as if this would make a difference: hoping that my inner energy would maybe, in some way, save him. Day after day, though, this fear was hanging around in my mind and I just could not shake it off!

I was off school, blagging it, cos I couldn't bother going to be truthful. Not that I admitted that, of course. I had just bought '5 minutes' by the Stranglers and the TRB 'Rising Free' E.P. These records remind me of this time. To take my mind off of things I was listening to these and doing a bit more drawing again creating another one of my D.I.Y projects... a fanzine/comic all hand-drawn stuff and felt tips and the like. The title was Clash- not surprisingly!

This particular morning, following a harsh bout of snow and freezing weather, all the pipes in our outside toilet expanded and burst. Our next door neighbour was called Annie and she was a classic character well loved by Mum, Dad and all who knew her. Her and her hubbie John would have made a TV sitcom between 'em. They were one of the funniest, down to earth, hat-full of swear words indulging, volatile yet colourful and endearing couples you could meet. John was a boozer, ex National service and hated it and all authority and a diamond geezer, as they say down South... a rough diamond, as anyone can say, and a good laugh with it: and he would fight anyone while yer at it! Annie was also salt of the earth and a right laugh: Proper working class Northern characters and all the better for it. My Mum thought the world of them. My Dad hated women swearing, without a doubt, yet Annie was the only woman that he would listen to swearing and just burst out laughing at her. If my mum had come out with a small portion of her vocabulary she would have been sent to Coventry, after a severe dressing down and a week's nagging at the very best.

The pipes were spouting and gushing water all over the show. I was off school but not too ill to go and have a look at all of the commotion. There they were me Mum and Annie with scarfs on their heads, fags in gobs and pinnies getting soaked through, trying to wrap old rags around these burst dry-docked submarines called water pipes. It was a sight to see, and there stood at the door, looking a picture of health, was my Dad stood upright, shirt sleeves rolled up, though not to join in the activity... laughing as loud as I had ever heard him. The air was blue from Annie and the water just flowed. My Dad stood there at the back door having the time of his life. He loved it. I was laughing at him laughing at them NOT laughing. Eventually the rags did the job and the water stopped, the tears of laughter still flowing from the scene's small audience. That story went down into my

Mum's story telling folklore for many a year and rightly so. The sad part of the story is that it was the last time any of us saw a glimpse of the Dad we knew, laughing and carefree and, most importantly, being able to breathe! I also didn't realise that I had been letting go of my worries and anxious dreams and had given up the cause. I felt I had to let go of them, don't ask me why. Over the many years since I have never been able to answer that question myself. I just let go one day and stopped feeding my worry.

It was a Friday evening: Feb 17th 1978. I was finishing off my Clash comic. My Mum was in the room. I don't think she had been to the bingo? Now that is serious. I know that there was only us and my Dad in the house. I went and sat with Dad and tried to talk to him; sitting at the end of the bed and telling him about my drawings and he was smiling, but not so much at what I was saying. Then he started to mumble, had some difficulty in his breathing and faded in and out of consciousness. He must be tired I thought. I stuck around just in case he needed anything.

After a while my Dad woke up and he was talking like I had never heard him before. I can't recall what he was saying, but it was obvious something was not quite right. I went and said to Mother in the other room "Some things wrong, Dad's saying stupid things, I can't make any sense of him, is he alright?" She went straight in to him and I could see she was very concerned. Before I knew it, Annie from next door was here too and she said "You had better go and get your Paul." Dad was, by now, asking for Paul. He was drifting away but was speaking every now and again. The ambulance came around 9.30pm just as our Paul appeared out of nowhere at the front door and Dad was being taken out to the ambulance. He winked at me as if to say "Alright kid, he's gonna be alright." I saw my Dad go into that ambulance that Friday night and that was the last I ever saw of him. My lasting memory is of him laid in that bed not being able to breathe!

That following day (Saturday) was a rush around for all of the family. It was a time of chaos and worry-etched faces. Our Dave, Steve and Michelle came down to stay at our house while the family went to see Dad. I could see on the adult's faces that this was serious, but no-one would admit it. We all tried to make out nothing was wrong and tried to do things to take our minds off it all, but it wasn't easy. The intense worry was clearly being felt by us all.

Early Sunday morning and me and the kids are woken up by our Paul and he gets our attention and tells us that my Dad (their Granddad) had gone. He had died a few hours earlier in hospital while we slept. The kids start to cry and I just felt numb. All I could think of was that I had let go of the worry: I should have known, why did I not do something. Why had I let go? What happens next? Will I see my Dad again? Is it my fault?

My Dad had now gone and the family soon dispersed. Our Glen was making plans to get married to his girlfriend, Lesley, the following year and our Paul and Megan were bringing up our Dave, Steve and Michelle. Everyone had their own lives to lead. I had changed over-night it seemed. My life certainly had. I wasn't a kid on a red chopper bike anymore that's for sure either. I now had a hell of a lot of growing up to do. I determined, to myself, that I would do it all alone and depend on no one but myself. Things were gonna also be hard for my Mother so I wasn't going to lean on her any more than I had to do: she was as determined too, in doing her best for me now as a one-parent family. She did all she could for me, in any shape or form that she was able, but the greatest thing she ever gave me... was allowing me to be myself, giving me the space I needed and making as many allowances for a angry, frustrated and rebellious teenager as any parent possibly could do under the circumstances. Most importantly, I was allowed to grow and boy was I ready for it!

By this time, we were well on our way to not being kids anymore, yet still at the age where what happens in life can either screw you up or strengthen you in later years to come. I reckon, looking back from today's perspective, the way my Dad's death affected me was a bit of both. For one thing, I know I did not really grieve properly at all. I simply put a brave face on and held back all of my mixed up kid emotions... pushing them further and deeper inside, so that it became something that I did not need to deal with. I can remember clearly, on seeing my Dad's grave - freshly covered with soil - for the first time. Our Glen had taken me, along with my mate Andy for some moral support. When I got to the cemetery, I was already feeling uneasy and wondering how I would feel. When I stood gazing at the grave, I felt a massive sense of disbelief and panic. It was a feeling that I was not at all familiar with and I did not like it one bit! I decided, there and then, that

I would not recognise this feeling, if I could call it that. I made my mind up to cast it aside, with all the rest of the emotional confusion going on in my head and not become friends with it in any form. In this way, whatever happened next in my life during the following years of being a teenager and all the pitfalls of growing up, every obstacle, no matter how large, would pale in comparison. I would quite easily be able to deal with anything life threw at me with little, if any, drawbacks if only I could get through this.

It was strange going back to school after losing my Dad. My mates were great with me... Andy had been upset on hearing about my loss, though us being lads we wouldn't admit this. My good school pal, Glen, who used to call for me every morning before school, was sound and supportive. I had only been away for a week; the funeral had been and gone and all was supposed to return back to normal. Back to routine then? I hate routines and mundanity! So much had changed within my life in so short a space of time. Routine and loss was my stalking ghost, music was my saviour!

Routine or not, things felt different. Well, I felt different anyway. My mates were still the same, the laughs still flowed and our interests, on the surface, seemed all intact and the same. The lasses were still bringing me colour posters of The Jam that they had torn out of their issues of Jackie and My Guy and me and Andy were still digging this new music we were becoming more enthralled by. But life felt so different... we weren't kids anymore. I had been forced to grow up in an unexpected way. I felt lonely, but strangely rejuvenated. I had to have something positive to focus upon.

School itself was too monotonous, the teachers were set in their ways, and they were bored and boring. Although I was at school most of the time, my mind was not on being there and what I should be doing. I learnt how to mask my inner thoughts and make out I was attempting to do my work. Honestly, almost all of what the teachers were trying to teach me was going straight through one ear and out of the other. The back of the class for a lark around was usually the best place for me. Some teachers left it at that, giving up any hope for me... and I really can't blame them. My school CV wasn't something that would impress many. School was right at the bottom of my list and music was right at the top!

In the next few months I immersed myself whole-heartedly into music: my saving grace was this music (Punk) that had attitude and spoke to me of rebellion. I had left behind my every other interest. The toy soldier regiments surrendered to various excitable kids and the last remaining comics didn't get read when they dropped through the letter box on a morning. The model paints and glue dried up as all attention turned to buying the exciting sounds of the New Wave and attempting to learn what the whole thing was truly all about. We got a brand new music centre to play our records and tapes on: it looked just like something that had been ripped out of the Star Trek enterprise dashboard and it was cool! The finishing touch was a record cleaning arm that soaked up all the dust off them as you played them: 'Tomorrow's World' had nowt on us then!

I heard that first Clash album that I had been staring at in the Sound of Music and it all changed for me. Yes it's a cliché that one, I suppose, but it's a true one. I never looked at things the same way again after hearing, feeling and figuring out the words and music to that massively influential and ground-breaking long player. Its influence and that of The Clash and Paul Weller and The Jam was firmly set in my head forever!

The 1970's were now speeding through their last few laps: the final two years (78-79) were unlike the previous years. The telly and popular culture and people's life styles was desperately hanging on to a tired old 70's kudos. 'Mind Your Language', 'Get Some In' and 'Love Thy Neighbour' being TV show examples of a well-worn path of 70's humour. Alf Garnett was being questioned for his bigoted morals and opinions and John Inman was still asking 'Are You free', whilst the arrival of comic revolutionary Wolfie Smith (played by Robert Lindsay) in 'Citizen Smith' signified a new breed of TV comedy icon, despite its obvious satirical slant. Amazingly a lot of the older generation who had travelled through the decade in typical 70's style and outlook, continued to hang on to their fashion look, attitude and dated ideals well into the next decade. Meanwhile the Punk generation and their younger juvenile siblings were responding to change and embracing new ideas whilst looking ahead. The 70's had been a colourful and often innocent experience and a real joy to grow up in but now the time had come to move forward. As the 60's Hippie dream had symbolically met its demise with the violence and negativity of Altamont at the end of that decade, so the 1970's ended with the arrival of Punk Rock and its Post Punk fall-out!

By now I had lost touch with some kids. Gary Mitchell moved off our street to a street not far away but our days of being proper mates had passed. Even though we still remained on good terms we went our own separate ways. Our days of fun together were over. Kids moved away, some went to different schools which may have well have been a foreign country to us at that age. The old fellas on the street – the Albert Tatlock and Alf Roberts look-alikes – started to pass away one by one and new people came to live on the street: new look-alikes appeared, Charles Branston, Alex 'Fibbin' Higgins and Lee Van Chuff moved in. Me and Andy Goulty would soon set off on our different paths through life. He, along with my other great pals, Pete Roddis and Shaun Angell, went down the pit after leaving school. Andy is now, ironically, a Headteacher. We have all tried our best to stay in touch over the many years that have passed since.

At the seaside, 1978: with our Steve, Michelle and Dave (and Francis)

I rode my red Chopper for the last few times that year. The decorations, stickers and the like on the bike had all been removed by now and I was starting to feel that bit self-conscious about being seen on the bike. I did have another bike made up by a fellow Punk-loving mate, Steven Doidge that Spring time: he sold it to me for three quid (yet again) and when I set off for a ride on it the bike literally fell to bits, parts were actually peeling away as I rode it. The thing fell to pieces in minutes, bolts n' all and left a trail of Bicycle debris in its wake. That was the last bike I ever owned.

Later that year another mate came and bought the Chopper bike off me for, you guessed it, three quid! The Scalextric went too, bit by bit, to another future Punk Rocker, Mark Barnet also known as the legendary Barney Rubble. He would turn up at the door with *cash for track* as me and my mates were getting ready to go Punking it up at the youth club and a bit later on our very first Punk Rock jaunts at the Sheffield Top Rank.

The sounds of the Jam were an obsession to me by now and everything to do with this new musical phenomenon at my disposal were being eaten up and integrated: the rebellious, the talented, great, the bad and the downright crap (and useless and ugly) of Punk Rock were firmly in my life and my journey had now truly begun!

....

So how has the world of the 1970's evolved for our generation of kids? What modern observations can we quickly pick up on? For a start isn't it weird how things change without us really noticing them right before our eyes and often end up back to front somehow. When I was young, the kids would be straddling rusty racer bikes handed down from their big brothers, bikes twice the size of them. Now you see over-grown chav teenagers riding small BMX bikes ten times too small for them! Cars in the 70's were rackety old Austin Morris and Hillman Avengers spread two to a street on average. Now you see chunky Military style four by four wagons that take up two houses drive spaces along with regular sightings of sports cars we only glimpsed of in James Bond films. From playing out battles with our regiments of toy soldiers on the back garden disappearing into a unknown world of war, bullets, spears and expressed miniature violence for us to a present generation of games console-intoxicated kids who indulge in a virtual reality of games that depict wars that are still actually going on around us in the world... all in ever-increasing authenticity. From plastic records in paper sleeves to invisible downloads and tiny machines that compile together the equivalent of decades of our record collections. It may all sound like teary-eyed nostalgia to some – and well some of it may be – but I for one feel damned lucky to have been around to experience those more primitive yet far more captivating, human and individual times.

Here we are in the 21st Century. That childhood vision of Dan Dare simulated; spaceman-inhabited machine-run future that we all naively imagined would be upon us far into the future is now here. In some ways a lot of it has come to be: computers running our lives, cameras following us everywhere, the high technology of our times and even the cloning of living forms. Meanwhile the kids of today communicate through the many mediums of the modern age and interact very little with each other in person... unlike our 70's generation of kids who shared so much together. What I am saying is that progress is great and I am all for it, but it does have a price!

I suppose the world will adapt and hopefully, one day will right itself. In the meantime I will take comfort in my memories and the people I care for, then and now, whilst making the most of the modern world's advances that I need, moving forward and forever learning as I go through life, but never forgetting my past. How could I possibly forget those days back in the 1970's, growing up in an ever-changing decade of fun, laughter and wide-eyed wonder? It's true that many of the people I shared those times with are sadly no longer around. The little gang I hung around with are spread far and wide and our lives have spread even further apart: but, as I said before, back then we all had one thing in common... we had a childhood to live through and experience... and live and experience it we did!

And to all those people that me and my mates pissed off, took the piss out of... seriously wound up and annoyed the hell out of! The teachers, the cops, the shopkeepers and lollypop women and most other walks of life.... Well, we were only kids; we didn't really mean any harm. Those people may be surprised to know that I have now grown up (in a fashion anyway). I suppose I turned out ok, though some may hold that to debate: I wouldn't stretch to saying averagely normal, but I ain't no criminal. But would I change all the daftness, misdemeanours and rebellious actions? Would I make amends and be a good boy? Would I heckers like!!! I would do it all over again... and with a gob-full of ear-crackling Space Dust I would loudly proclaim - to quote my dear old departed Mother - 'with brass knobs on too!'

Acknowledgments -

Spelling mistakes (by me) Homework done mostly on time by me, Proofing by Paul Jespersen

Book backed, sealed and designed by David Spencer

Photo extracts from Action and Battle comics are used with permission from the copyright owners, Egmont UK Ltd.

Victor and Warlord comics kind permission of D.C.Thomson & Co.Ltd

Rawmarsh Market photo of 1965 used by kind permission of The Francis Frith Collection

Chopper bike images and related text used with kind agreement of Raleigh bicycles at Raleigh.co.uk

For support- Sheffield Star, South Yorkshire Times, Rotherham Advertiser

And thanks to the following people... John Quinn, Sally Burton, Andy Coles, Jane Salt and Stuart Hastings at Sheffield Star archives section, Tim Jones, Gary Mitchell, our Paul, our Glen, our Megan, Dave, Steve, Michelle and Lesley, Shaun Angell, Rob Wasteney, Carl Day, Melanie Leggett, Joan Rainbow, Bill McLoughlin (DC Thomson), Paul Jespersen, Carl and Margaret Eggleston (for the groovy 'Sound of Music' photos), John South, Heather Quinn, Marsha and Rob Armitage, Sonia Brookes, Kevin Igoe and everyone who has shown interest in my work.

R.I.P Russell Brookes

A Massive thanks for the constant support and faith... Vanessa, Dean and Sean.

All effort has been attempted to establish the authorship of all photographic and written material contained within this book. If anyone feels they should have been acknowledged please contact me and all credits will be respected within further editions

Continue the journey with these other books by the same author

'Our Generation'

'Out of Control'

'This is Our Generation Calling'

Available from all good book shops and online at

www.ourgenerationpunkandmod.co.uk

EXCITING
NEWS!

COMING SOON FROM 'DAYS LIKE TOMORROW BOOKS'

A FURTHER RIDE THROUGH THE DECADES WITH

'CAN'T STAND THE 80'S'

(By Tony Beesley)